It gives me great pleasure to endorse Dr. Angie Corprew-Boyd's newest book. Dr. Boyd explores a topic of great concern to the body of Christ. This book is sure to propel the body of Christ to begin a thought-provoking, heartfelt dialogue about the emotional aspects of working within ministry and stewarding relationships. The message will release untold levels of pain that have been bottled up for generations in the church.

—Dr. K.W. Brown
Senior Pastor
Mt. Lebanon Missionary Baptist Church
Chesapeake, Virginia

In my travels as a minister and teacher of God's Word, I meet so many people at home and abroad that fit the following description: "I love God, but I hate church!" There is a reason for this new growing population in God's kingdom. The reason is church hurt—wounds received in and at the church! Dr. Corprew-Boyd has been assigned by God to masterfully address this sensitive, unique, and surely necessary issue in the body of Christ. Are you wounded? Read it! Have you wounded someone? Read it! You cannot remain the same. Dr. Angela uses her skill as a writer to bring information, hope, and healing. Thank you for living it, writing it, and making it available.

—Dr. Wanda A. Davis-Turner
Preacher, Teacher, and Author

If you haven't experienced church hurt, keep going to church! If you need to be free from church folk, read this book.

—Aretha Olivarez
National Speaker, Nonprofit Consultant, Author, and Entrepreneur

This is another brilliant book in the anointed works of Dr. Angela Corprew-Boyd. Church Hurt is positive indication that God does not seek just visitation, but rather habitation. He wants to inhabit every phase of the believer's life. Dr. Boyd marvelously illustrates that if we who are broken go to the top of the mountain, we will be gloriously changed. However, if we stay at the foot, as Aaron did, we will only receive a shadow of His healing power and glory. This book will empower and encourage believers everywhere. Thanks, Dr. Boyd, for a book of such incredible wealth.

—Junious Epps Jr.
Author of *Everybody Plays the Fool*

CHURCH HURT

CHURCH HURT

DR. ANGELA L. CORPREW-BOYD

CREATION HOUSE
A STRANG COMPANY

CHURCH HURT by Angela L. Corprew-Boyd
Published by Creation House
A Strang Company
600 Rinehart Road
Lake Mary, Florida 32746
www.creationhouse.com

Scripture quotations marked NW are from *The Webster Bible* by Noah Webster, Ada, MI: Baker Publishing Group, 1988.

Scripture quotations marked ASV are from the American Standard Bible. Copyright © 1960, 1962, 1968, 1971, 1972, 1973, 1975, by the Lockman Foundation. Used by permission.

Scripture quotations marked RYL are from *Young's Literal Translations* by Robert Young, 1989. Reprinted by Baker Book House, Grand Rapids, Michigan, copyright © 2003.

Word definitions from *Webster's Unabridged Dictionary*, New York: Random House, 2003, unless otherwise marked.

Cover design by Dana Drake, preppypoodledesigns@yahoo.com

Library of Congress Control Number: 2008923868
International Standard Book Number: 978-1-59979-371-9

08 09 10 11 12 — 9 8 7 6 5 4 3 2 1
Printed in the United States of America

From the sole of the foot even unto the head there is no soundness in it; but wounds, and bruises, and putrifying sores: they have not been closed, neither bound up, neither mollified with ointment.

—Isaiah 1:6

DEDICATION

This book is dedicated to my husband, Reggie,
and our three angels:

Devin Jared

Donovan Jaye

Dawn Janae

*For he shall give his angels charge over thee, to keep thee
in all thy ways.*

—Psalm 91:11

ACKNOWLEDGMENTS

F IRST, I GIVE honor to my Lord and Savior Jesus Christ, who is the giver of life! I thank Him for allowing me to write this book. May it be a healing source to the pastors, ministers, evangelists, elders, prophets, apostles, bishops, and lay members who are still experiencing pain from wounds of their present and past.

I also thank God for my husband, Reggie, and our three children, Devin, Donovan, and Dawn, as well as for their undying love and patience. Thanks to Prophetess Aretha Janine Olivarez and Rev. Dr. Patricia Coker-Bell, who continued to encourage and inspire me when times were good and bad and for confirming the contents of this book; to my spiritual leaders for their constant prayers and guidance, which helped me realize my season; and to all those whom God appointed to give personal testimonies and reveal what He will do after wounds have been mended properly and completely.

Finally, to my beloved churches: Revelation Tabernacle Worldwide Ministries and First Baptist Church, Berkley, both in Norfolk, Virginia, and Philadelphia Fellowship in Chesapeake, Virginia. Thank you for all the experiences that have caused me to grow and be the anointed woman of God that He predestined me to be. Through love, I learned to love you. Through pain, I learned to love you. Through rejection, I learned to love you. Through hurt, I still learned to love you. And now I love you even more. Thank you for loving me.

Thank you, Father Pat Umberger. Your words saved my ministry! I thank God for using you to speak life and heal my open wounds.

I thank God for every episode and issue He allowed in my life, because they became the manuscript for this book. He was pulling out of me the treasures that would escort me to my destiny. Thank you, God!

CONTENTS

THE HEART

(A PERSON'S INWARD LIFE, INNER SELF, INNER BEING, MIND)

In the Bible the word *heart* refers to both the major organ of the body (Lev. 17:11) and to the most important part of a person, that is, to man's innermost being. The heart is the central part, the very center of a person's life. It is the most vital part of a person's being.

The heart lies deep within, containing the *hidden self* or *real self* (1 Pet. 3:4); that is, the heart contains what a person really is, his true character. The heart determines what a person does, his behavior, whether good or depraved (Matt. 15:18; Mark 7:21–23).

1. The heart is the source of a person's rational being: reasoning (Mark 2:6), understanding (Matt. 13:15), and thinking (Matt. 9:4).

2. The heart is the source of a person's emotional being: joy (John 16:22; Eph. 5:19), afflictions (Luke 24:32), and desires (Matt. 5:28).

3. The heart is the source of a person's spiritual being: conscience (Acts 2:37), will (Rom. 6:17), faith (Mark 11:23; Rom. 10:10), and evil (Matt. 15:18; Mark 7:21–23; cp. Jer. 17:9).

Source: *Practical Word Studies in the New Testament*, Copyright © 1988 by Alpha-Omega Ministries, Inc., Volume 1, page 1013.

PREFACE

CHURCH HURT IS a very difficult topic to discuss, especially when you have experienced it. People, Christians in general, do not like to admit that someone could be hurt or wounded instead of helped in the church. The purpose of this book is to allow the wounded to recognize they are not alone and that they are still the talented, anointed men or women of God who have been called by Him.

> *The hurt you have experienced will not deter you from your purposed future, if you won't allow it. It's really up to you. It's not too late.*

The Christian community has been the product of abuse from those who deem themselves shepherds over God's sheep. I'm not categorizing *every* church, pastor, teacher, prophet, evangelist, or apostle as one who beats up on his or her congregation. That's the last thing I would do because I love with a deep passion and appreciation those who have been called by God to declare His Word and shepherd His sheep. I have, however, experienced much hurt in the church by numerous men and women, not all shepherds, who say they love God but whose actions speak a completely different story. I have seen it and experienced it both from afar and up close and personal. Because I am called upon to minister and give personal and spiritual counsel to countless men and women who have experienced church hurt, I felt a personal desire to share what—or rather, who—saved me from my deepest wounds. Furthermore, my personal desire was to avoid allowing the hurt that I experienced to hinder my ability to be an effective witness for the Lord.

Some may question my motives, "Why is she writing this book?" I had to, for my own personal healing and for countless others who have allowed church hurt to drive them away and keep them from fulfilling their God-given purpose. It's not too late for you. You must first realize that some of the churches that we attend are dysfunctional and imperfect. Why? Because dysfunctional and imperfect people attend them. Even so, that does not give you the excuse to escape why God planted you there. Your prayer should be to ask God to give you the patience and wisdom to deal with whatever challenges you face. That's what I did, and that's why I am still a part of a church family. Is it perfect? No, because I'm there and I'm imperfect, as are many other imperfect people.

There are imperfect people throughout the Bible. Because the Bible addresses every circumstance, situation, problem, or question we may have, I decided to seek God for an answer to why people who desire to live godly in Christ will suffer persecution or church hurt. I came to realize that even in the Old Testament there were people who hurt others while in the church. Look in 1 Samuel 1:3, 7, and 9–11 (NLT), and you will find the following account:

> *Each year Elkanah and his family would travel to Shiloh to worship and sacrifice to the LORD of Heaven's Armies*

*at the Tabernacle. The priests of the LORD at that time
were the two sons of Eli—Hophni and Phinehas.... Year
after year it was the same—Peninnah would taunt
Hannah as they went to the Tabernacle. Each time,
Hannah would finally be reduced to tears and would
not even eat.... Once after a sacrificial meal at Shiloh,
Hannah got up and went to pray. Eli the priest was
sitting at his customary place beside the entrance of
the Tabernacle. Hannah was in deep anguish, crying
bitterly as she prayed to the Lord. And she made this
vow: "O LORD of Heaven's Armies, if you will look upon
my sorrow and answer my prayer and give me a son,
then I will give him back to you. He will be yours for his
entire lifetime, and as a sign that he has been dedicated
to the LORD, his hair will never be cut."*

This is a prime example of church hurt. Hannah could
have walked out of the tabernacle wounded for life. Instead
she went to the tabernacle—church—and prayed. She went
to the place where the presence of the Lord was, where the
fullness of joy was, and called on Jehovah. She was bitter in
her soul, but instead of leaving the church, she went to the
church.

When I read these verses, God gave me an astonishing
revelation. There are people who will know your situation
and still be jealous of you. Like Peninnah, they will poke fun
at you, taunt you, talk about you, and try to make you fearful
based on what they think they know about you. Yes, the Lord
had shut Hannah's womb, but it was for Him to get the glory
for what He was about to do: show His grace and favor upon
her life.

God will use people to provoke His purpose out of you. How? In verse 7 the scripture reveals that Hannah went to the tabernacle, the house of the Lord, and there the adversary provoked her. Now, it is obvious that the enemy is lurking in the tabernacle "seeking whom he may devour" (1 Peter 5:8). And if the enemy can provoke you to give up what God has already purposed, then he has won.

Your answer today is, go to the tabernacle and pray. Make a vow to God. Let the enemy know that instead of being provoked to walk away from the promise, you are walking into it. Pray it into existence.

There are many other examples in the Old Testament and the New Testament of church folks hurting one another. This was just one story that transformed my thinking and saved my life and ministry from the wounds of church hurt. I pray that upon the conclusion of this book, your wounds will be healed and you will get back to where God positioned you to be—walking in your gifts and calling in the body of Christ.

From the sole of the foot even to the head, there is no soundness in it, but bruises and sores and raw wounds; they are not pressed out or bound up or softened with oil.

—Isaiah 1:6, ESV

A man's spirit will endure sickness, but a crushed spirit who can bear?

—Proverbs 18:14, ESV

Let not your heart be troubled: ye believe in God, believe also in me.

—John 14:1

PERSONAL NOTES

CHAPTER 1

NO LONGER BOUND

*And ye shall know the truth, and the truth
shall make you free.*

—John 8:32

I CAN TRULY SAY that the unadulterated Word of God, who is Jesus the Christ, has made me free. Through His ministering angels, God has allowed my wounds to be healed, thereby allowing my spirit to be made free: "If the Son therefore shall make you free, ye shall be free indeed" (John 8:36). Since my inner being, mind and soul, has been set free, I can minister to others without causing pain and transferring my wounds to them.

I'M FREE!

It has taken me seven years to write this book. Why has it taken so long to finish? In the Bible the number seven represents divine completion or perfection. During the last seven years, God was still preparing me to not only experience my story, but to come out of it. This book could not have been completed until I was healed of every episode that caused me to have the vision to write the book. I had to experience the wound, acknowledge the pain, and be delivered.

On July 1, 2004, the prophetic word came from a dear friend and colleague, the Reverend Dr. William D. Tyree, III. He said, "From trial to triumph to testimony...What good is victory if you can't share it?" He may not have coined the phrase, but it was much needed at the time. Thank you, William! I'm ready to share my victory with the world.

IN THE BEGINNING

One night seven years ago, God came to me in a deep sleep and brought before me the book of Isaiah in a dream. This was especially meaningful to me because I greatly admire Isaiah the Prophet. I regard him as one of the most powerful models of leadership in the Bible. I have always considered him to be a great prophet to a great nation, one who spoke with a holy boldness.

In my dream, God used Isaiah to address the church of today, comparing it to Judah. The people of Judah were in denial and refused to admit their sins, and because of their denial—their revolt and rebellion against God—they continued to suffer. What God revealed to me was a vivid account to which we can relate.

When any of us continues to deny our sins and refuses to admit our need of God's cleansing and forgiveness, we often suffer. For example, if we experience the pain of a headache and continue to ignore that we have it, it only worsens if we do not tend to it. The result could be as simple as being moody and frustrated toward others or as severe as not being able to fully concentrate or focus on the task at hand. Before long, the headache is responsible for short responses, days missed from work, and a negative attitude. Instead of dealing with the pain and getting the medical attention we need, we continue to handle it ourselves until we pass out and someone else notices and comes to the rescue. When we dismiss the headache as something minor after it has been persistent for days, weeks, or months, we have taken matters into our own hands. But what if it's not just a headache but an aneurysm; not just loss of memory, dizziness, high blood pressure, heart palpitations, stress, or fatigue but really a stroke. The symptoms of a near-fatal crisis have persisted and taken control while we're in denial of the true pain. God wants us to know that in His presence we can safely begin to come out of denial and deal with truth. We can begin to see an end to suffering. But to do that, we must trust Him to bring us healing and deliverance.

I thought about the church and how many have made choices and lived their lives contrary to what God instituted and established for His glory. As I thought, I saw the vision of a people sick and hurting, bruised and wounded, yet trying to "walk worthy of the vocation wherewith ye are called" (Eph. 4:1). People weren't getting better—they were getting worse. They were attending church, but they were still hurt. They were hearing the word but still hurt. They were even operating in their gifts but still in pain. They were a part of every ministry but still wounded. In fact, they were even ministering to the sick and shut-in but were still troubled themselves.

God wanted to fix it. I heard the Lord asking, "Whom shall I send, and who will go for us?" as in Isaiah 6:8. Like the prophet Isaiah, I proclaimed to the Lord that night, "Here am I! Send me." And He said, "Go" (Isa. 6:9).

The word the Lord gave me to share was Isaiah 1:6: "From the sole of the foot even unto the head there is no soundness in it; but wounds, and bruises, and putrifying sores: they have not been closed, neither bound up, neither mollified with ointment."

I asked what He wanted me to share with the nation about this scripture. When He spoke, the vision was clear: that passage is a metaphor for the human body. It illustrates the physical corruption of the body when it—or rather, the person—is in a state of denial, revolt, and rebellion. As the scripture plainly amplifies, when we're in this state we're sick from head to toe. And not just physically; there is no soundness in our thinking, no logic, no stability. There are only wounds, bruises, and putrefying sores.

What's putrefying? The diseased and dying tissue that is decomposing. In Isaiah 1:6, wounds and bruises are a metaphor for problems, hurts, and issues. Unhealed, they fester and die. The tissues decay and decompose. Simply stated, they rot. And they smell foul. If you're suffering from spiritual illness and decay, then you stink too. The smell is a spiritual malodor in your heart, your soul, and your spirit. You don't need actual deodorant or perfume from the drugstore to cover the scent; you need the ointment from the Word of God. But you aren't aware of it. Why? Because you've been walking around with those open wounds for so long that they have become part of you. You've stopped noticing them as something wrong.

You have become numb to them. This is how God showed me the people in the church. Is that you? The more wounded you are inside, the more you try to cover up. The more you try to cover up, the more exposed you become. You are no longer undercover, but open to the world to see. Everyone begins to notice the wound except the wounded individual. When someone has been in pain a long time, he or she does a good job of "covering" by acting out in certain ways—for example, as the clown or the harmless flirt or other familiar types. This is really the pain acting out, the results of the wound. Maybe that's not you, but perhaps you're an active alcoholic or struggle with an addiction to pornography that you keep hidden. However it is expressed, if your wounds are deep and long-term, you can be certain that they are affecting your behavior, your life, and the lives of others in concrete ways. Wounds begin to manifest and become out of control when they are exposed. "They have not been closed, neither bound up, neither mollified with ointment." Is that you?

What does *mollified* mean? It refers to wounds that are soothed, subdued, alleviated, relieved, or lessened. Wounds that are being healed. In fact, the word *mollify* comes from an ancient Latin word meaning "to soften."[1] That's exactly what oil does. It softens and heals. God's anointing oil—the Word of God who is Jesus the Christ—mollifies and heals. Although Isaiah was sent to warn Judah thousands of years ago, this scripture has a message for the church today as well. As I began to read the scripture in my dream, I heard the Lord say, "This is happening to the church, the body of Christ." Since we are a body, when one of us, one part of the body, is hurt, it spreads to the rest of the congregation until the whole body is contaminated and in pain. When that happens, church, it's time to be healed!

ON ASSIGNMENT

Before God gave me my assignment, He had to deal with me on an intimate level. I came to the conclusion that He wasn't looking for people who were perfect or who pretended to be perfect. He was looking for someone who could say what Isaiah said: "Lord, I'll go! Send me!" I, Angela Corprew-Boyd, followed. If you are willing to turn your past failures and wounds over to God, He will not allow them to stand in the way of His plans for you and your future. It has already been predestined, and He will not take it away from you.

As one of God's chosen vessels, I know what it is to stand before God's people to declare the Word of truth. I also know what it feels like to teach the Word, prophesy, preach and proclaim God's truths, and bleed on the inside. I know what it's like to lay hands on someone, and the pain in me is so tremendous that I feel death on the inside. I know what it is to not be totally free because of wounds not healed from my present and my past. Once *self* was out of the way, I came to a terrifying conclusion while I was in prayer early one morning: I had been ministering the Word in pain. I had been preaching the Word in rejection. I had been prophesying the Word in hurt. All I proclaimed in the name of Jesus was my suffering from the open wounds that had never been mended—and these were not sufferings for the cause of Christ. But today, I declare I *am* free!

As a minister, preacher, evangelist, prophet, or teacher of the gospel, have you ever found yourself in the same situation as I've described? If so, as you minister, prophesy, teach, and preach, you've been allowing your spiritual and emotional wounds to hinder you from receiving the fullness that God has predestined for your life. And to take it further, you may have hindered those you're ministering to, or you may have enabled them to lose sight of what they should have received. Why? Because you have not reached a point where your wounds are completely healed.

How did I begin this process of healing? Acknowledgment was my key. Realizing and acknowledging I was wounded and needed God immediately was my plea and my prayer. When we envelope ourselves in prayer, God will show Himself mightily.

God spoke clearly that morning as I was in prayer, and now I speak clearly to you. God wants you to be completely healed. If you continue to minister in pain, in hurt, in rejection, and in denial, your ministry will not be complete. Your members will lie dormant. Your vision will be stagnant. Your destiny will not be fulfilled. And your life will not unveil as God has predestined. In other words, you and your purpose will never reach their full potential. God wants you to acknowledge that your open wounds from the past are spewing blood from the pulpit to the pews and from one pew to another because the wounds were never properly tended.

If you want to embark on the journey to rid your spirit and your heart of the wounds that have been inflicted on your life and move to another level of productivity in the natural and the spiritual realms, this book is for you. If you truly want to see open wounds mended, healed, and closed properly, this book is for you. If you want to see growth in your life and that of your family, your church members, and your ministry, this book is a must for you.

This book will share the following with you: the many issues that have caused hurt (open wounds), which leads to dormancy in the body of Christ; how hurt has been transferred to church members by preachers; and what to do to be completely healed. An end must come to the wounded trying to heal in the church, and wounded healers must take their place for the church.

God has allowed me to prophetically write this book because His Spirit grieves over those who are hurt in the church, great men and women who are not walking in their purpose and gifts. This pain is contrary to the reason He purposed the church, and we have strayed completely from His purpose. The church was created as a means of giving the lost—those who are sick because they know Him not—a place of refuge and healing. God is calling for the church to position itself to get back to its original purpose. In that effort, He wants pastors, preachers, teachers, evangelists, prophets, deacons, trustees, and lay members to unmask and come clean! Do what He has called you to do with a clean heart. He reminds us in Romans 12:1–2:

> *I beseech ye, therefore, brethren, by the mercies of God, that ye present your bodies a living sacrifice, holy, acceptable unto God, which is your reasonable service. And be not conformed to this world: but be ye transformed by*

*the renewing of your mind, that ye may prove what is
that good, and acceptable, and perfect will of God.*

He wants you to be completely healed from your past and
move expeditiously to your predestined future. Allow Him
to do it.

From the sole of the foot even to the head, there is no soundness in it, but bruises and sores and bleeding wounds; they are not pressed out, or bound up, or softened with oil.

—Isaiah 1:6, RSV

A man's spirit will endure sickness; but a broken spirit who can bear?

—Proverbs 18:14, RSV

For as he thinketh in his heart, so is he...
—Proverbs 23:7

PERSONAL NOTES

_____

_____

_____

_____

_____

_____

_____

_____

_____

CHAPTER 2

INFLICTION AND INFECTION

M ANY MINISTRIES AND churches have evolved from inflicted pain. These ministries were not established because it was the season for the ministry to begin or because God spoke it into existence, but because pain was the driving force to do better or be better than the ministry the individual left.

God's chosen men and women have gone through much hurt since entering the church world. Much of this hurt, which is related to our spiritual and emotional state, causes us to be bound to our present state without having a glimpse of our predestined future. Though it may seem surprising, because of that spiritual and emotional hurt, we have not and cannot move from that level of hurt and pain to deliverance, healing, and freedom. And so we move to a level of denial that causes more spiritual and emotional stress when those initial inflictions are brought back into our awareness.

Many people don't want to acknowledge this because they fear others' opinions and because the hurt is so great and unbearable. This hurt has such a physically powerful effect that it makes choices for you—and sometimes the choice of last resort is to leave the ministry or church, thinking that doing so will make the pain just disappear. But it does not. It stays no matter where you go because you have not dealt with it properly. You haven't given it to God.

Whenever you see the people you feel are responsible for those wounds, the pain comes back. When a wound is left unhealed, every time you have to address issues that are close to what caused your spiritual and emotional wounds and the resulting discontentment, sorrow, and discomfort in your life, you experience a flashback of the issue or the people who inflicted the pain. For example, what happens when you see someone you haven't acknowledged as a source of your wound? You disregard them, discount their very being, because it's too difficult to address them and the situation that caused the hurt. You walk away. We all do. We don't try to reason with them. We don't even talk about it. But remember, the Bible tells us to "forgive, if ye have ought against any: that your father also which is in heaven may forgive you your trespasses" (Mark 11:25) and commands us to "come now, and let us reason together" (Isa. 1:18).

Why do any of us, as Christian men and women, anointed and appointed by God Himself and who have a relationship with God, fail to allow His Word to work in our lives? It's because we have embraced the issues, circumstances, problems, and people that caused us to be hurt and allowed them to escort us, once again, to a level of denial. These wounds will repeatedly resurrect themselves until we let God address them properly so that they, and we, can heal. How much longer do you want to live this way? Isn't it time to face and confront your open wounds?

FROM THE PULPIT TO THE PEW

If you are a preacher reading this, know that the issue isn't just inside you. What about the church leaders under you? The members? The rest of the congregation? They feel the same pain from the open wounds of the great man or woman God has chosen to pastor, minister, teach, prophesy, and lead them. Why do they feel their preacher's pain? Because many churches and ministries were established out of pain, and that pain seeps from the pulpit into the lives of the people. Instead of preaching through your pain, your pain is being preached. This pain has caused deep wounds that have festered and spread from ministry to ministry and church to church because you continue to carry it. Isn't it time for you to heal the pulpit and make it free? Isn't it time for the pews to be healed, delivered, and made free?

Through His Word and in His infinite wisdom, God allows you to know and understand that "He sent his Word, and healed them, and delivered them from their destructions" (Psalm 107:20). If you don't allow God's Word to heal you, you will cause your own destruction. The pain that was inflicted upon you and caused your wounds should no longer hinder you if you have allowed the Word to heal them. Now is your time to seek total deliverance and to understand what these wounds are and how they have delayed your destiny.

As I began to seek God about my pain, I became more transparent. It was as if He placed my life on an X-ray machine. I could see myself when I began my ministry and the storms I struggled through to get where I was. One main image I saw repeatedly as He showed me my past was the church. I found myself reminiscing about the churches God had planted me in and how others inflicted pain in my life. That's when God began to show me the open wounds and the bleeding that continued to stagnate my ministry. At that point, I asked for understanding from God. He showed me that the wounds had hindered me and prevented the fullness of my ministry from going forth. I didn't understand and had to ask Him, "What's a wound?" From there, the conclusion I came to was easy. The wound is an unresolved issue that I've allowed to inhabit my being.

In fact, I realized I had two wounds: a spiritual one and an emotional one. When I would show up for church Sunday after Sunday, I would leave the same way I came—wounded. My heart was disheartened, therefore blocking the spiritual food that would escort me to freedom and wholeness. Because my heart possesses both my spiritual and emotional being, I could not grasp the empowered word that was coming forth to set me free. It was then that I knew if I was to be set free, I had to confront my wounds. But first, God had to define *wound* for me before I could begin accepting what I needed to do to be healed. Now allow me to help you. Let's start by looking at these terms and their definitions.

- *Wound:* (1) an injury involving the cutting or tearing of the flesh; (2) an injury or hurt to the feelings; (3) to inflict pain upon; (4) to hurt someone's feelings, pride, emotions and/or self-esteem

- *Spiritual wound:* (1) an injury involving the cutting or tearing of the soul; (2) an injury to someone's spirit or state of mind; (3) to inflict a pain upon the inner person (soul); (4) to hurt or damage the holy or immaterial frame of mind

- *Emotional wound:* (1) an injury involving the cutting or tearing of someone's feelings or emotions; (2) to hurt or damage someone's emotions, expression or passion.

- *Self-inflicted wound:* an injury someone causes to him or herself

- *Inflicted wound:* any injury one person causes or inflicts on someone else

These definitions should help you to realize you have been wounded and recognize the wound that you are carrying. Many circumstances have transpired in ministries and churches that have inflicted wounds, but they have not been addressed or completely healed by God, though the Bible says that "with His stripes we are healed" (Isa. 53:5). The problem is that many people don't have the tenacity of faith to believe that "with God all things are possible" (Matt. 19:26). If you have the faith to believe it, then it shall come to pass.

When wounds are confronted or treated when first inflicted, the pain is not as severe or prolonged. Early healing leads to feeling good, living well, ministering without guilt, and being a more powerful witness in the body of Christ. For example, if you have been rejected in a relationship and you feel useless and unwanted, then you need to admit that to God and yourself. In the process, you need to also share your pain with the person who caused it. Stop pretending that it does not exist and that you are just fine. Exposing your pain is what you need to do to receive healing. When you confront the fact that rejection has caused a wound, you are ready to deal with it head on. Don't wait until you become numb and bitter. When you confront your wound in its infancy, sharing your testimony of deliverance is more powerful. You're able to come to the house of worship and praise God for your deliverance and healing.

On the other hand, what happens if wounds aren't confronted and treated when they're first inflicted? What happens if you walk around for days, weeks, months, and even years with untreated, open wounds? They become infected. And they stay infected. And, as mentioned, the infection spreads.

But it shouldn't, and it doesn't have to. As your mediator and healer, God is giving you an opportunity right now to confront the issues that caused your wounds. When you begin to take inventory of your wounds, you will see that your entire being has been affected.

How long can you afford to keep those wounds alive? When a wound is left untreated and persists, issues derive from it and begin to overtake your life. An issue comes from the result of your wound—your problem, your hang-ups, your vexation, your pain, your flaw, your mistake, your malfunction, your disobedience, your anxiety, your break-down, your weakness and/or your hindrance. They become strongholds, and scripture tells us, "For the weapons of our warfare are not carnal, but mighty through God to the pulling down of strong holds" (2 Cor. 10:4). A stronghold is anything that exalts itself above the Word of God. For example, you know that Jesus came so that you could have abundant life. If you are not living an abundant life, if your life is just fair, then your situation has exalted itself above the words of Jesus. If you say, "I can do all things through Christ which strengtheneth me" (Phil. 4:13), and you are still in a relationship with a person who is not your husband or wife, that stronghold, the affair, is exalting itself above the scriptures. It's basically saying that God's Word does not work, but the stronghold does. It lingers, festers, and contaminates until it becomes deadly. That stronghold is the issue that comes from your wound.

When that happens, your spirit and your soul become affected. For example, the woman with the issue of blood's life was affected because of the law. Leviticus 15:19–27 confirm that a woman with an issue is affected greatly. These scriptures indicate that a woman who has an issue of blood shall be put apart for seven days (v. 19); whoever touches her shall be unclean until evening; everything that she lies upon shall be unclean (v. 20); everything that she sits upon shall be unclean; whoever touches her bed shall wash his clothes, bathe, and be unclean until evening (v. 21); whoever touches anything that she has sat upon shall wash his clothes, bathe, and be unclean until evening (v. 22); if the woman's issue continues beyond the seven days she shall remain separated as long as it continues (v. 25); whoever touches any of the things she contacts during that time shall be unclean (v. 27).

Clearly, the stronghold from this wound, her issue, affected not only her solely, but it affected her husband, children, church, and vocation as do our wounds today. Thus she allowed it to exalt itself above God's Word, Jesus Christ. How does she allow her issue to be a stronghold? For twelve years she sought physicians for healing. She allowed her trust in man (physicians) to supercede her trust in Jesus, which led to prolonged sickness.

There was no excuse for her to give in to physicians. The Word of God confirms His power in Matthew 4:24:

> *And his fame went throughout all Syria: and they brought unto him all sick people that were taken with divers diseases and torments, and those which were possessed with devils, and those which were lunatick, and those that had the palsy; and he healed them.*

When we don't follow the plan of God, we are sure to delay our wounds from being healed. Not only do we see this now from the woman with the issue of blood in the New Testament, but it is also chronicled in the Old Testament.

Prior to Jesus' coming under the Mosaic covenant, the steps that the woman with the issue of blood followed would have still contradicted the Word; for at this time, Jews were subject to the Mosaic covenant to seek God for healing (Exod. 23:25).

According to 2 Chronicles 16:12–13, King Asa sought his healing as the woman with the issue did in Matthew 9:20–21. The Bible states:

> *And Asa in the thirty and ninth year of his reign was diseased in his feet, until his disease was exceeding great: yet in his disease he sought not to the Lord, but to*

the physicians. And Asa slept with his fathers, and died in the one and fortieth year of his reign.

Death fell upon him because of his disobedience to God.

When He declares in Psalm 107:20, "He sent his word, and healed them, and delivered them from their destructions," He literally meant that He sent His Word, His Son! (See John 1:1.) Furthermore God's desire to heal is evident in the messianic prophecy in Isaiah 53: "But he was wounded for our transgressions, he was bruised for our iniquities: the chastisement of our peace was upon him; and with his stripes we are healed" (v. 5).

That the woman's healing finally manifested after twelve years allows you to witness that He is Jehovah-Ropha, your healer. The question is, when do you plan to call Him? When do you plan to trust Him? Has your issue distracted you from who He is in your life? Stop calling on doctors who don't know your diagnosis or prognosis. Call on Doctor Jesus, who knows your issue, your circumstance, your disease, your failures, your desires, and your purpose. When you go from physician to physician, girlfriend to girlfriend, homeboy to homeboy, pastor to pastor, or church to church, you are repeating the actions of the woman with the issue of blood. Luke 8:43 says that after twelve years of this illness, she "had spent all her living upon physicians, neither could be healed of any." They can't heal you! Stop expecting other people to give you what you need. Only your Creator can do that.

The Spiritual Wound

A spiritual wound is a wound that affects or afflicts your mind. Your spirit is your intellect; it's your conscience. It makes your decisions to go left, go right, and do the right thing or the wrong thing. It's your will. If your will is affected by a wound, then you're not in a position to make a rational decision. The Word says, "God hath not given us the spirit of fear, but of power, and of love, and of a sound mind" (2 Tim. 1:7). You didn't have a sound mind. It was full of grief, depression, oppression, past hurt, pain, and anything else that bombarded it when you wanted to go forth.

I know there have been instances where your spirit was wounded in the church. Maybe you announced your call and were told, "You're not ready," or that God couldn't have called someone like you. Maybe you were just trying to operate as a member in the body and someone said, "Why did she come here?" Perhaps you were asked to lead a Bible study or be the worship leader, and when word of it got around people didn't show up or the pastor openly embarrassed you because he didn't understand your gift. In these and similar situations, you may have been spiritually wounded, stifled in your ministry because of someone's jealousy or lack of knowledge. When that happens, you begin to perish.

When people say or do things to hurt your spirit, the effect will last until you release their words or action from your thoughts. We all know the cliché "Sticks and stones may break my bones, but words will never hurt me." That's a lie from the pit of hell. Sometimes the very words that have been spoken into our lives cause our spirit to be crushed. The Bible shares several scriptures that describe the potential conditions of an individual's spirit.

In Genesis 41:8, we read that the pharaoh's spirit was troubled. Exodus 6:9 says Moses' spirit was in anguish. Numbers

5:14 tell us we can have a jealous spirit. In Deuteronomy 2:30, the king's spirit had been hardened by the Lord. Psalm 51:17 mentions a broken spirit; 1 Samuel 1:15, a sorrowful spirit; 1 Chronicles 5:26, a stirred up spirit; and Ecclesiastes 1:17, a vexed spirit. When your spirit is disturbed and your flesh is making decisions, you are not willing to allow God to heal you. What is the condition of your spirit right now?

THE EMOTIONAL WOUND

An emotional wound affects or afflicts the soul. These wounds are most difficult to see. You hide them behind a fake smile, a fancy suit, an education, or a position in the church. These wounds are not visible to the naked eye. You can't see the wounds because the wounded individual covered them so well and has become accustomed to hiding them. In time, the wound becomes almost a part of the person, and he or she feels almost comfortable with the pain after having been afflicted with the wounds for so long.

SOUL OUT

The effects of that emotional wound will manifest in your soul. You see, your soul is made of your feelings, emotions, passions, and desires. It exercises your mental faculties. Since that's the case and since your actions are based on how you feel, how you feel will determine how you act.

In other words, your emotions are manifested through your actions. As your emotions are stimulated, your body reacts. For example, the Bible says, "My soul shall make her boast in the Lord" (Ps. 34:2). You make your boast when you clap your hands, or stomp your feet, or open your mouth with a voice of triumph coming forth—or all three at the same time. The psalmist is bragging about how he and all of us react when we have feelings for and about God. You know that when you react to your emotions, something visible or observable begins to happen on the outside. But if your emotions are damaged, it's almost impossible to react to how God makes you feel. If that's the case, the wound has succeeded in overwhelming your emotions, and you can't praise God the way you want.

From the sole of the foot even to the head [there is] no soundness in it; but wounds, and bruises, and putrifying sores: they have not been closed, neither bound up, neither mollified with ointment.

—Isaiah 1:6, NW

The spirit of a man will sustain his infirmity; but a wounded spirit who can bear.

—Proverbs 18:14, NW

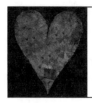

Jesus saith unto him, Rise, take up thy bed, and walk.
—John 5:8

PERSONAL NOTES

_____

_____

_____

_____

_____

_____

_____

_____

CHAPTER 3

THE DEBILITATIVE EFFECTS

P AUL WRITES TO Timothy and warns that in the last days men will be found, "Having a form of godliness, but denying the power thereof: from such turn away" (2 Tim. 3:5). Paul encourages us to be vessels fit for the Master's use even in perilous or difficult times. A form of godliness is an outward appearance of reverence for God. Denying its power describes the religious activity that is not connected to a living relationship with Jesus Christ. When wounds become debilitative, we are controlled by them. Our praise and worship become hindered, and we act the part of worship. It's a form of godliness.

When we enter into His gates with thanksgiving and into His courts with praise (Ps. 100:4), it seems that we should be expecting something from God. We go to worship with the forethought that whatever burden may have tried to take control of us will certainly be released in worship.

But why doesn't it always happen? It doesn't happen because we fail to enter with thanksgiving and praise. We enter with wounds, and we expect someone else to take on what we brought in—and that makes us spiritual leeches, parasites attached to someone else's anointing or someone else's praise. We try to become excited by feeding off someone else's worship, praise, or testimony instead of entering into the spirit realm ourselves; so we leave the same way we came in—hurt, and still in pain—because we haven't turned to God to heal the wound and set us free.

And so it continues. The wounds we carry debilitate us. They have long-lasting effects that hinder our worship, our praise, our consciousness, and our judgment. We have become used to carrying these wounds to the point that we're comfortable in what was once an uncomfortable situation for our spirit. The wounds have us bound. They keep us stagnant. They set us up to be misjudged, misconstrued, and misunderstood. When this happens, it seems as if we're identified by our *condition* instead of our God-given purpose. These wounds debilitate us to the point where they may seem to define our being.

I'M IN PAIN, AND I CAN'T GET UP

Are you ready to stop playing church, to stop showing up wounded and leaving the same way? Are you ready to stop accepting defeat and be more than a conqueror? Are you ready to overcome fear, shame, guilt, embarrassment, depression, rebellion, despair, or even that comfortable ache by the blood of the Lamb and the very words of your testimony?

You may begin your day with the awareness that it is the day the Lord has made (Ps. 118:24) and with the conscious intent to rejoice and be glad because you have made up in your sanctified mind that you will not leave the church same way you entered. Yet despite what you said, you leave with the same problem, the same issue, the same situation *because you didn't let it go.* We become stars in our own dramas because we know how to be counterfeit worshipers. We continue to perform our own one-act play in spite of our intentions, and we still leave the church in pain because of the wound. And we've done it long enough.

It's simply a meager, vain form of godliness we exhibit when we go before God with open wounds that have not been healed. How can God receive true worship when we are still in pain from our past? He can't and won't if it is not true worship! Matthew 5:23–24 states it clearly: "Therefore if thou bring thy gifts to the altar, and there rememberest that thy brother hath ought against thee; Leave there thy gift before the altar, and go thy way; first be reconciled to thy brother, and then come and offer thy gift." Because our pride gets in the way of us being obedient to the Word, we continue to present ourselves bound when we come to worship. But it is counterfeit, a form of godliness God does not acknowledge. This debilitates our worship, our praise, our prayers, our preaching, our teaching, and our walk with Christ.

You may be asking yourself about the wounds that have resurrected themselves from your present and your past, questioning what they are and where they came from. These wounds, which tend to make their presence known, are deeply rooted. Is it a reminder that the people of God let you down? Every now and then we are reminded of them when we see the scars that were left. What are these scars?

Scar: (1) a mark that is left on the skin after a wound, scratch, cut, abrasion or burn has healed; (2) a mark made on a surface by scratching or scraping; (3) a permanent effect on a person's mind, character, or countenance made by some painful experience.[1]

Our emotional scars are the result of wounds, cuts, abrasions, or scratches that have been inflicted on our souls. The scar is a constant reminder of a more complex condition inside us, the wound, which had to evolve because of the pain or hurt that was endured. For example, when a person has open-heart surgery, the surgery leaves a permanent mark internally and externally. No plastic surgeon can ever completely remove the result of that operation. However, the memory of the pain and operation can be soothed if the scar that resulted in the pain is properly tended. The memory of your pain from an emotional wound can also be soothed if it's properly tended. The scars from your wound can be used for the glory of God if they are allowed to heal fully.

When you look at that scar, what do you see? Is it a reminder that you are still depressed? Is it a reminder that you were rejected? Is it a reminder that you are still bitter and resentful toward the person who caused you pain? No matter how minor you think your wound is, it still causes pain, especially when you have to see it and wear it every day. A cut, an abrasion, a scratch, and a burn are metaphors for emotional and spiritual wounds. Just as the physical wounds leave a visible reminder of the deep hurt that you have endured, so do the non-physical wounds, emotional and spiritual. Let me help you diagnose what kind of wound you have.

Cut: (1) to penetrate or divide with or as if with a sharp edged instrument; (2) to hurt the feelings of severely;

(3) to refuse to recognize socially; to snub; (4) to lower, diminish or reduce

Abrasion: (1) a scraped spot or area, as on the skin; (2) the act or process of scraping, rubbing, or wearing away

Scratch: to mark or damage the surface of by rubbing or scraping with something sharp or rough

Burn: an injury caused by heat, abnormal cold, chemicals, etc. and characterized by redness

Do you recall the pain of a wound, cut, abrasion, scratch, or burn? A paper cut is sometimes not seen with the naked eye, but the pain that results from it is a prolong sting that hinders you from wanting to use your hands until it's properly tended. After a day or more, you may continue to feel the cut, but it's still not always visible. It's the pain from the paper cut that you remember. That's how a wound from a personal cut is, too. Someone may ignore your presence or dismiss you from a conversation or even fail to acknowledge your worth. That's a cut that leaves a scar, a cut you won't forget.

Acknowledge the wounds that still exist in your life. Take a look, examine them, figure it out—be the determiner. Which ones tunnel through your many coverings and unveil their residue as a reminder that they're still living and festering inside you? Which ones are wounds that someone inflicted on you, and which are self-inflicted? This is the first step in the healing process. We must follow the psalmist's model and say, "I acknowledge my transgressions: and my sin is ever before me" (Ps. 51:3).

When we look back to biblical times, there were men and women who had been wounded. What type of wound surfaced for the woman in Luke 13:10–13? She was known by her condition of being bowed over for eighteen long years. The Bible says she had a spirit of infirmity and could "in no wise lift herself" (v. 13). That spirit of infirmity had a debilitative effect on her mind and her body. It was her spirit that was wounded. A person's spirit is the invisible force of the intellect. It's the will, mind, or conscience of the individual that compels him or her to make sound choices. Infirmity is a weakness of human nature. It could be an ailment, imperfection, shortcoming, disorder, inferiority complex, or some inadequacy that we may have developed about ourselves based on what someone else may have said about us.

Simply put, it's an issue. And an issue can be considered as a wound when it's not tended to properly. When one analyzes the definition of *spirit* and *infirmity*, you conclude that it was a condition of her mind that debilitated her. As the physical body lives and recognizes pain through nerves, the spirit being also lives. The spirit is the place where we connect with God because He is a spirit. Had she connected with God, her spirit would have been strong and empowered, causing her to be lifted up. If her spirit had been strong enough, her mind could have clearly received the healing and truth of God.

An infirmity is a weakness of our human nature. It is the feebleness of mind and body, malady, frailty, disease, sickness, weakness.[2] The infirmity that enabled her from physically standing up also kept her bowed down. In her mind, she was not stable enough to grasp the Word of God, for she saw only her condition. She could not in her mind think of herself as healed, "for as he thinketh within himself, so is he" (Prov. 27:3, ASV). She could not mentally perceive herself as whole. Her mind kept her bound.

Her spirit was wounded, causing her to be bowed over. After eighteen years, she had learned to be comfortable in an uncomfortable situation. Her wounded state of mind and body kept her from being whole. But one day, she became sick and tired of being known by her wound. When you become sick and tired of being called out by your condition instead of your God-given name, you will be ready for God to heal your wounds.

The woman in the scripture made something happen by acting on what she knew. I would think that she knew who Jesus was because she recognized His voice while passing by the synagogue as He was teaching. She was captivated by His teaching and found herself in proximity of the Messiah. She knew she was wounded! She knew she needed to be healed! She knew she needed deliverance, and the only one who could deliver her was Jesus Himself. She made her way to the place where her condition could be changed.

Many times we are wounded and comfortable right where we are because we have been there for so long. People don't know our names. They just know us by our condition—the woman who was bowed down for eighteen years, the girl down the street who had a baby out of wedlock, the man around the corner who drinks, the deacon who is having affairs with women in the church, the preacher who mistreats his congregation, the sister who isn't married, the woman who had five husbands and was looking for the sixth. When we are wounded, people don't call us by name, they call us by our condition because we have attached to it and it's become familiar to us as well as others. It's time to let go and allow Jesus to heal your condition, just as He did for the woman in Luke 13:10–13.

If you follow her steps, you can be on the way to recovery. First, she was acknowledged as being wounded (she had a spirit of infirmity, v. 11). Then she got up from her pity party, her depression, her disappointment, her rejection, her low self-esteem and went to the synagogue.

What have you done to get His attention? I believe out of her belly flowed a praise that provoked Him to see her and her condition. After seeing her, the process of her healing began. The Bible gives a three-step process: (1) He called her to Him; (2) He spoke to her: "Woman, thou art loosed from thine infirmity" (v. 12); and (3) He laid hands on her. It's as easy as one, two, three. What are you waiting for?

No one says the process feels good. Sometimes acknowledging the wound causes excruciating pain, and if it is not dealt with properly it can be deadly. But understanding pain is the best first defense. To understand pain, let's start with a basic definition.

> Pain: the sensory and emotional experience associated with actual or potential tissue change[3]

Thus, pain not only includes the perception of an uncomfortable stimulus (cause) but also the response to that perception. In medical terms, there are three levels of pain: acute, persistent acute, and chronic. Acute pain from a wound tells you something is very wrong. Persistent acute pain, because it's ongoing as well as intense, may actually interfere with the healing and recovery process. And when pain persists beyond the expected time required for healing, it becomes chronic.

To fully understand pain, you must have experienced it. If you have experienced pain, then there must have been a wound. If you are still experiencing pain, there must still be a wound from a cut, an abrasion, a scratch, or even a burn. Which type of wound are you still carrying?

YOUR CONDITION

When you allow your condition to overwhelm you, you have given the debilitative effects of the wound control. Your condition may be a wound from birth. You may blame your pain on someone else. However, that does not mean you should stay wounded. God has given you the ability and resources to be healed. Look at the man in John 5:1–9 who sat outside the pool of Bethesda. The Bible tells us that this infirm man associated himself with others who were wounded (v. 3), people who were impotent, blind, lame, and even withered. There are always people who have wounds more serious than our own. We seem to subconsciously attract people worse off than we are in order to feel better about our situation. As the saying goes, misery loves company. How can you be helped by another wounded person? You can't! You must rely on Jesus Christ to heal you. Put yourself in the way of Jesus, and He will come to see about you.

Jesus recognized that He came to earth so that the man would have life and have it more abundantly, but he had been living beneath his privilege for thirty-eight years. He was stuck in his wound. When Jesus asked him, "Wilt thou be made whole?" (v. 6), the man first replied with excuses: "Sir, I have no man, when the water is troubled, to put me into the pool: but while I am coming, another steppeth down before me" (v. 7). Jesus has asked you that question, too, but you continue to give excuses. What's your excuse?

YOUR SEPARATION

> *Who shall separate us from the love of Christ? shall tribulation, or distress, or persecution, or famine, or nakedness, or peril, or sword? As it is written, For thy sake we are killed all the day long; we are accounted as sheep for the slaughter. Nay, in all these things we are more than conquerors through him that loved us. For I am persuaded, that neither death, nor life, nor angels, nor principalities, nor powers, nor things present, nor things to come, Nor height, nor depth, nor any other creature, shall be able to separate us from the love of God, which is in Christ Jesus our Lord.*
>
> —Romans 8:35–39

No external force can separate us from God's love, but that doesn't mean we are incapable of separating ourselves from God. I learned this when God asked me, "Who shall separate me?" Before I could answer I heard Him say, "Wounds." As I thought about it, I began to realize we allow our wounds to separate us from our healer, Jehovah-Ropha, Jesus Christ. Other people cause the wounds, cut us, scratch our feelings, and made us bleed. Other people burn us with nasty looks or contrite attitudes. Other people hurt us deeply. But other people do not and cannot separate us from God. However, we alienate ourselves from God when we hold on to our wounds, refuse to forgive those who wounded us, and remain unhealed.

Stop where you are, lift your hands to the Lord, and pray out loud:

> *Lord, I forgive those who hurt me, and I ask You to heal all my wounds. I give all my hurts to You, and I receive healing right now. I thank You that I am more than a conqueror through Jesus Christ.*

Now, if you believe it, shout, Glory! Amen.

You are battered from head to foot—covered with bruises, welts, and infected wounds—without any soothing ointments or bandages.

—Isaiah 1:6, NLT

The human spirit can endure a sick body, but who can bear a crushed spirit?

—Proverbs 18:14, NLT

Forebearing one another, and forgiving one another, if any man have a quarrel against any: even as Christ forgave you, so also do ye.

—Colossians 3:13

PERSONAL NOTES

CHAPTER 4

RESENTMENTS

WHAT HAPPENS WHEN we continue to allow wounds from church hurt to fester and burden us? We become resentful towards those who hurt us. And when we become resentful, that means we have been overcome by another issue due to the wound not being healed. I became bitter and resentful toward the people who inflicted my wounds. I was overcome by bitterness, and vision for ministry began to dwindle. When I finally became sick of masking my bitterness—hiding behind a smile or a preached Word—I asked God to help me with my resentment toward several people I felt had violated my trust. He did!

In my healing process, the Lord directed me to a Web site that chronicled my healing of resentment. I want to share it with you in hopes that you will receive it and get on the road to being healed. It comes from Father Pat Umberger, a Roman Catholic priest who is the pastor of St. Patrick Parish, Diocese of LaCrosse, Wisconsin. Father Umberger says:

> *The Latin root of the word resent connotes feeling something again, as in hanging onto it with our teeth and*

fingernails, and feeling it over and over and over.... Jesus tells us we must forgive our brother or sister from our heart. Earlier in Matthew's Gospel, Jesus speaks again about forgiveness. "Peter came and said to Jesus, 'Lord, if another member of the church sins against me, how often should I forgive? As many as seven times?' Jesus said to him, "Not seven times, but, I tell you, seventy-seven times" [Matt. 18:21–22]. It's not easy to do, that's for sure. We can often find it in our hearts to forgive those we love, but it's harder to forgive those we don't particularly care for. Resentments don't go away all by themselves, and they have great power.

The Recovering Community shares this wisdom with us: "This business of resentment is infinitely grave. We found that it is fatal. For when harboring such feelings, we shut ourselves off from the sunlight of the Spirit. The insanity of alcohol returns, and we drink again. And with us, to drink is to die."—Alcoholics Anonymous, p. 66. According to one of the co-founders of Alcoholics Anonymous, "Punishment never heals. Only love can heal." Bill W., Letter, 1966.

Be angry, and sin not: let not the sun go down upon your wrath: Neither give place to the devil.

—Ephesians 4:26–27

RESENT SOMEBODY

The moment you start to resent a person, you become their slave. They control your dreams, absorb your digestion, rob you of peace of mind and good will, and take away the pleasure of your work. They ruin your spirituality and nullify your prayers. You cannot take a vacation without them going along! They destroy your freedom of mind and hound you wherever you go. There is no way to escape the person you resent. They are with you when you are awake. They invade your privacy when you sleep. They are close beside you when you eat, when you drive your car, and when you are on the job.

You can never have efficiency or happiness. They influence even the tone of your voice. They require you to take medicine for indigestion, headaches and loss of energy. They even steal your last moment of consciousness before you go to sleep.

So if you want to be a slave, harbor your resentments.

RESENTMENTS HARM US

It becomes apparent that our resentments harm us even more than those we resent. They're so powerful that they don't go away when we have no further contact with the one we resent. They can remain with us even though the person has died long ago. If we consider someone we resent even for a few seconds right now, we can upset our entire equilibrium. Our blood pressure will go up, and we can get ourselves into such a state that it's hard for us to know what to do. So how can we best handle those resentments?

There are many things it's best not to do. It doesn't do us any good to rehearse the resentment. Going over it in our heads hundreds of times simply gives that person more power in our lives. Plotting revenge isn't particularly effective, either. The more we think of the situation, the worse we feel. If our thinking is not going to result in any action, then it's fruitless.

It can be very helpful for us to pray the Serenity Prayer. Here it is:

God, grant me the Serenity to accept the things I cannot change, the Courage to change the things I can, and the Wisdom to know the difference.

ACCEPT ... CHANGE ... KNOW

Now we can consider the things we need to accept. If the person doesn't like us and shows no willingness to look at us in any other way, then it's fruitless to try to make the person like us. Many people express anger not because of what we've done, but because they're angry people with issues of their own. There are many things we cannot change. We certainly can't change that! We don't need to allow the issues of others to upset our equilibrium and become our issues. We have very little power over other people, places or things. We can give the situations we can do nothing about to God, and allow God to take care of them.

Resentments are like stray cats. If you don't feed them, they'll go away!

There are some things we can change. We can certainly change ourselves and our own reactions to those who have harmed us. We can change the words we use to describe what happened from "terrible" or "horrible" to "unfortunate"—we can't deal with things that are "terrible" or "horrible." Those are out-of-control words. "Unfortunate" situations can be dealt with and then left behind. Many things are "unfortunate." Things become "terrible" or "horrible" only when we let them.

We need courage to change what we can. Perhaps that means making peace with the person involved. We clean up our side of the fence. Perhaps we'll go to the person we resent and apologize for our part in the difficulty. We must do that with absolutely no expectation that the person will return the favor and apologize to us, as well. If we've done real harm, it's a good idea to celebrate the Sacrament of Reconciliation, the Catholic sacrament often called "Confession." In the traditional church, the Bible suggests in Matthew 5:22-25 that "one is to go to thy brother and be reconciled." That would be the honorable act to perform to move past the pain of being hurt by someone. If we've added to the problem through judgment and gossip, we can express sorrow for that, as well. What goes around comes around. Our unkind words will come back to us and bring unhappiness to our lives.

Become Willing

We can suspend judgment. A wise person once said, "To understand everything is to forgive everything." We can give the person who has harmed us the benefit of the doubt. We can pray for them. We can pray that they receive all the good things in life we'd like to have ourselves. We can pray that they become so deliriously happy that they don't feel the need to hurt anyone else. We can pray this prayer without condition and without asking anything for ourselves. When negative thoughts return, we can pray the Serenity Prayer, and then a prayer for the person we resent.

We certainly need to have the wisdom to know what we can change and what we can't. It's not good for us to give up too soon. We can seek God's wisdom during our times of prayer, as well. Then it's best to concentrate first on things that can be changed. God can do for us what we could never do for ourselves. If we try all these things and still find we're resentful, then we've done all we can do by ourselves. It's time to turn our resentment over to God. How do we do that?

Pray for the willingness to let go of the resentment. It's not a good idea to set a time limit for when we'll let go. It's not good for us to decide what it will feel like after we've let go. It's not good for us to figure out when and how God should work. We simply pray for willingness. We can say, "God, help me become willing to let go of this resentment." It's a prayer that we might do this "someday." It might be a year or twenty years from now, or five minutes, five hours or five days. Time is not our concern. We just need to become willing to let go.

They Melt Away

And our resentment will simply melt away. When it's happened, it will have been effortless. We'll have trouble even giving God the credit, and it will have been so natural and easy. God will do for us what we cannot do for ourselves. We just need to let God do that.

Resentments are certainly troublesome. We're not off the hook until we let others off the hook. As we pray so often in the Lord's prayer, "Forgive us our trespasses as we forgive those who trespass against us." We must act on what we say and feel.

Father Umberger's words of wisdom helped me process exactly what I was feeling. I had to ponder several questions, so I ask them to you: Do you have bitterness or resentment toward someone who inflicted pain on you? Do you have bitterness or resentment toward yourself because of poor decisions that had debilitating consequences? Accept, change, and know that you can be healed by the power of the Holy Spirit. All you have to do is speak it, then have faith to believe it.

Once I became truly willing to release my bitterness and resentment, I was no longer defeated by my wounds. I had to release something in order to receive something; when I released bitterness and resentment, I received forgiveness myself and I was able to forgive. I am now at peace, and my past wounds are healed.

Do what I did! I opened my mouth and began binding sickness from my wounds and loosing healing for my heart. I have that much power working in me. (See Ephesians 3:20.) The Word of the Lord declares, "Whatsoever thou shalt bind on earth shall be bound in heaven; and whatsoever thou shalt loose on earth shall be loosed in heaven" (Matt. 16:19). Once you realize there is life and death in the power of the tongue (Prov. 18:21), you will begin to speak healing to your wounds. It certainly worked for me!

From the sole of the foot even unto the head there is no soundness in him; wounds, and weals, and open sores: they have not been dressed, nor bound up, nor mollified with oil.

—Isaiah 1:6, DT

The spirit of a man sustaineth his infirmity; but a broken spirit who can bear?

—Proverb 18:14, DT

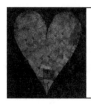

When Jesus saw him lie, and knew he had been now a long time in that case, he saith unto him, Wilt thou be made whole?

—John 5:6

PERSONAL NOTES

CHAPTER 5

HEALING HIDDEN WOUNDS

H OW MARVELOUS GOD is! I hope you begin to allow resentment and bitterness to be released from your spirit. If you haven't yet released it, maybe you pulled the bandage off as a start to the healing. Prayerfully, these words will transform and heal the wounds.

This chapter is a message preached by a dear friend of mine, the Reverend Dr. William D. Tyree, III, the pastor of First Baptist Church, Berkley, in Norfolk, Virginia, while I was in the process of writing this book. After hearing the CD on Sunday, July 9, 2006, I knew God was still up to something. It was predestined to be the fifth chapter of this book. I give Him praise for the Reverend Dr. Tyree. Here is his message.

HOW GOD HEALS HIDDEN WOUNDS

How many of you have ever had a broken bone? More than one broken bone at one time? How many of you have ever had stitches? More than thirty stitches? How many of you have ever had surgery of any kind? How many of you have ever had a knife wound? In the kitchen or a dark alley? How many of you have ever had a gunshot wound? How many of you have ever been wounded in a war?

Today, I want to talk with you about how God heals your hidden wounds. Not the physical, but the hidden wounds. Hidden wounds are the memories that still hurt, those recollections from your past that when you think about those things they still cause pain in your life—memories of abandonment; memories of abuse, whether it is physical, spiritual, emotional, or sexual abuse; memories of ridicule; severe criticism or hatred or prejudice or criticism that has just torn you down. Where do you get the hidden wounds of life? They come from everywhere, from society, the prejudices in society. And some of you have felt that. You can certainly get them from family members, and those are the ones that hurt the most, from parents, from kids, from brothers and sisters, aunts and uncles. You can get them in the work place. You can certainly get them on the school-yard from mean children. And you can get them from the church. They're everywhere.

As a pastor, I've talked to people, and I've learned two truths about life. One is that everybody has a hidden wound. You may be masking it, but everybody has a hidden wound, at least one. It may include but is not limited to an emotional scar from somebody in the past who hurt you in some serious way. The other thing I've learned is that emotional scars take longer to heal than physical wounds. People have gone to Vietnam and other wars and come back. Their bodies would heal, but sometimes it would take years and years to get over the emotional scars. However, the good news is this: Jesus Christ wants to heal your hidden wounds. You can start on that process today.

Allow me to help you. In the Bible, God gives Himself different Hebrew names describing the benefits to us. One of them is in Exodus 15. He says, "I am Jehovah-Ropha," which means "I am the God who heals." The Bible also says this in Psalm 147: "God heals the broken-hearted and bandages their wounds." You may ask, "How does He do that? I'd like to have my hidden wounds healed—those hurts and recollections of the past, memories." Since you have asked how, here are the steps in God's healing process.

When you look at the life of Jesus, you see He healed a lot of people, physically and emotionally. There are certain patterns and principles that come up over and over again in the way He dealt with people. They don't always go in this order, but you can find these five principles in God's process of healing of memories.

Five Principles, Five Steps

Step 1: Reveal my hurt.

You're never going to get well until you face your feelings straight on. The Bible talks about the problem of stuffing it down inside and not talking about it. Psalm 39: "I kept very quiet but I became even more upset. I became very angry inside, and as I thought about it, my anger burned." He's saying that holding on to hurts is like carrying hot coals in your heart. You're the one who's going to get burned. Hidden wounds, when you try to stuff them down, don't heal. They fester. And pushing a hurt aside doesn't get rid of it—it just makes it worse.

Some of you are tired all the time. One of the causes (not all of them) of constant fatigue is that you're using up emotional energy on resentments, grudges, guilts, and griefs of your past. You use so much energy dealing with those things that you have no energy for the present. So you're tired all the time. The Bible says, "When I kept things to myself, I felt weak deep inside me and I moaned all day long." He's saying it's emotionally draining.

Because we live in a sinful world, people abuse other people. I have no doubt that someone else has abused many of you in some fashion. It's amazing how people respond to abuse in different ways.

> *Some people try to respond to abuse by just forgetting it. "I'll just put it out of sight, out of mind, and stuff it."*

> *Some people try to run from it. There are many ways to escape—get drunk, do drugs, go to bed with people you don't even know, or get (too) involved in work.*

> *Some people try to just ignore it.*

> *Some people try to pass it off on somebody else. They blame others.*

> *Some people try to cover up their abuse. For some reason, we feel guilty. We think it's our own fault. We don't want anybody to know, so we push it down. It's like a Coke bottle that you've shaken up—it's about ready to explode. One day the top is going to come off.*

> *None of those ways works.*

Step one is to be honest about your pain, about your fear, about your anger, about your resentment and bitterness over what people did to you, about the way you felt when you were abandoned or abused, ridiculed, and the shame that maybe you felt. You've got to start by revealing your hurts. You've got to be honest. Honest with whom? Three different people: First, you have to be honest with yourself. You have to own up to, "This hurts! I'm ashamed of this," or "I still hurt over this."

Second, you have to be honest to God. You say, "God, this is how I feel!" and you vent and let it all out. God can handle that. God already knows how you hurt because He saw it when you were hurt. And He hurt with you and He grieved with you. It's not going to surprise God when you're honest to God about the pain in your life and the shame in your life. You're not going to surprise Him. He already knows. He already cares. He already loves you. He just wants you to be honest with Him. It's for your own benefit—kind of a catharsis, getting it out.

Third, be honest with at least one person you trust. Tell somebody with skin and bones. There's something healing about revealing your feeling to one other person. The Bible says in Job 18:4, "You are only hurting yourself with your anger." When you stuff it down, you're only hurting yourself. If you don't have anybody you trust, we have lay counselors where you can share in a trusted situation. You need to start getting this out and getting it off your chest. You're never going to get well until you reveal your hurts.

Step 2: Release those who have hurt me.

You can't get well as long as you harbor resentment. For your own sake, you've got to let go of your right to get even. The fact is, you only have x amount of emotional energy, and you're going to spend it in some way. One of the most difficult decisions you've got to decide in life is, "Do I want to get well or do I want to get even?" You can't do both. You're going to have to decide that: Do you want to get well? Or do you want to get even? You don't have enough emotional energy to do both.

Let me share a secret with you: Getting even will not take away your pain. Some of you have done that. You've been able to get back at the person who hurt you. You know it didn't solve the problem—you still feel the pain.

There's only one way to get rid of hurt in your heart when somebody's hurt you: forgiveness.

You say, "But they don't deserve to be forgiven!" I didn't say they did. You're right; they don't. Neither do you deserve to be forgiven, but God's forgiven you. I'm not saying forgive them because they deserve it. I'm saying forgive them for your own sake. You can't get on with your life as long as you're stuck in the past. As long as you hold on to resentment, you are stuck. That person is still controlling your life in the present, even though they may have been out of your life for many years.

Jesus certainly understands abuse. He was abused. I suggest you do what Jesus did. Jesus had twelve wounds right before He died. Six were physical, and six were emotional.

The six physical wounds

He had head wounds from the crown of thorns.

He had face wounds when they smote Him.

He had back wounds from the whipping they gave Him.

He had hand wounds from the nails.

He had foot wounds from the nails.

He had side wounds from where they stuck a spear in His side.

It didn't just stop at the physical wounds. He also experienced emotional wounds. Some of us can relate to these because we have been there. We have been emotionally wounded on the job, in the home, in relationships, and in the church. Yes, in the church. I believe the deepest wounds in Jesus' life were the hidden wounds, the ones you could not see. He had six emotional wounds.

The six emotional wounds

He knew betrayal.

He knew verbal abuse.

He knew abandonment.

He knew rejection.

He knew hatred.

He knew injustice.

 Jesus could have blown them all away in an instant. Instead, He stretched out His hands and said, "Father, forgive them. They don't know what they're doing." Why should I forgive those who hurt me? One, God's forgiven you. Two, you're going to need more forgiveness in the future. Three, it's the only way you're going to get well. There is no other way. You've got to release your right to get even. "When Jesus suffered, He did not threaten to get even. He left His case in the hands of God."

Step 3: Replace old tapes with God's truths.

 Your brain is like a tape recorder. It has recorded every single experience your five senses have experienced—everything you've smelled, everything you've seen, heard, touched, tasted—it's all in there. Everything people have said. Your brain is an amazing recorder. It has recorded it all down, good and bad, right and wrong, true and false.

 Here's the problem: your brain doesn't distinguish between things that are true and things that are false. Particularly when you were a little kid, there were some things that were said to you that were flat-out lies, but you believed them. And if you believed them, you acted on them. Some of you are still operating on faulty data. When you base your life on faulty data, then what happens is that you build a self-defeating lifestyle. You

63

set yourself up for failure and pain and hurt. Some of you, when you were kids, had adults or authority figures in your life say things like, "You're stupid...You're ugly... You're never going to amount to anything...I'm embarrassed to call you my child... You're uncoordinated... You're dumb... Why can't you be smart like your sister/brother?" On and on. They said things to you like, "You're worthless," and that went into that recorder.

Some of you are twenty years old—thirty, forty, fifty, sixty—and you're still acting on old tapes and wondering why you still do things that defeat you. These are self-defeating actions and habits. You've got to replace those tapes with God's truths. Romans 12:2 says, "Let God transform you into a new person by changing the way you think." How does God change us? How does He transform us? By changing the way we think. How do you do that?

First, you have to pray and say, "God, would You heal my memories? Those things that hurt, those open wounds in my heart? They still hurt. Would You heal my memories and begin that process?"

Second, you need to fill your mind with God's Word, the Bible. The more you fill your mind with His Word, the more it will start erasing old tapes and putting God's truth in your mind. You need to get into this His Word. That's why we say come to mid-week Bible study, get involved in a Sunday school class, and have a daily quiet time. The more you get in His Word, the more you build your life on truth, and the more you replace all the lies. You fill your mind with His Word by memorizing and studying and reading.

Third, you must believe the truth about you. What is the truth about you, anyway? What has God said about you? "Through what Christ would do for us [there's the key!] God decided to make us holy in His eyes, without a

single fault we stand before Him covered with His love."
That's how God sees you, "without a single fault." Once
you step across the line and give your life to Christ, He
sees you "without a single fault." He takes everything
you've ever done wrong—the guilt, the regrets, the
shame, and the hurts—and He erases it and says, "We're
going to start over." God sees you without a single fault.
Because you're really that way? No. But because of what
Christ's love has done for you. That's the good news.

Psychologists have proven over and over again that
the way you see yourself—your self-esteem, your self-
worth, your self-concept—is largely determined by what
you think the most important person in your life thinks
about you. The way you see yourself tends to be based
on what you think the most important person in your
life thinks about you. So I want to suggest to you that
you make Jesus Christ the most important person in
your life—because He's going to tell you the truth. So
you have to decide: Am I going to listen to liars ("You're
worthless! You're nothing!") or am I going to listen to
what Jesus Christ said?

Now, what has Jesus Christ said? The Bible says when
you are in Christ you are valuable, you are acceptable,
you are lovable, you are forgivable, you are capable,
and you are usable by God. That's what God says about
you. So the question is, what are you going to believe?
What somebody lied to you about? What somebody told
you on the school ground? What some imperfect, sinful
authority figure said to you? Or what God says about
you?

It's your choice. You have to replace old tapes with
God's truth.

Step 4: Refocus on the future.

Get your attention off your past and onto God's plan for your future. This is one of the real problems with a lot of therapy that's out there today. There are many, many popular therapies that deal with healing of memories, regression into your past, and things like that. If the counselor is not a Christian and if the counselor is not basing his or her therapy on the principles of God's Word, run as fast as you can away from that therapy! If you get involved in that therapy that is not biblical and godly-based, you will end up worse off than you are right now. I could give you lots of examples of people who had a painful past, went to a secular counselor, did not follow God's standard of healing but went according to Freud or somebody else or some pop psychology, and they're worse off than they were when they went. Run from it. What it does is get you so focused on the past that you get stuck in it and you can't get on with the present, much less the future. You go further and further back, back, back, and then you are just stuck there.

There are three steps to refocusing on the future. They're all in Job 11 (from the Good News translation): "Put your heart right, reach out to God and face the world again, firm and courageous. Then all your troubles will fade from your memory like floods that are past and remembered no more."

#1. "Put your heart right." That means give up your right to get even. Release those who have hurt you. Forgive them, whether they deserve it or not. You do the right thing, whether they did the right thing or not. You say, "I don't feel like doing that." Do it anyway! Because it's the right thing to do, and it's the only way you're going to get well. Do it anyway. Put your heart right. You do the right thing, which is forgive.

#2. "Reach out to God." You need to ask Jesus Christ to come into your life, and you need to ask Him to begin healing your hidden wounds, and you need to ask Him to start bringing good out of the evil that has happened to you. Here's the real issue: do you really want to get well? If you do, you stop focusing on your hurt and you start focusing on your Healer. Stop focusing and getting obsessed with your hurt and the people who hurt you, and start focusing on your Healer, Jesus Christ. Jehovah-Ropha—"I am the God who heals you." He is the answer. Nobody else is.

#3. "Face the world again." Don't withdraw. Don't pull yourself back into a shell. Resume living. Stop saying, "I'm a victim!" Start saying, "I'm victorious!" Start looking ahead.

If you follow these steps, notice what happens: "Then all your troubles will fade from your memory. Like floods that are past and remembered no more." Wouldn't you like that? Wouldn't you like to have your troubles fade from your memory? Then take these steps. The principle is that "forgetting is caused by refocusing." You don't forget the past by saying, "I'm going to forget it! I'm going to forget it!" What are you doing? You're thinking about it the whole time. It doesn't work that way. You refocus on Jesus Christ and His plan and purpose for your life, and you become so consumed and committed to it that you don't have time to think about the past. It's refocusing.

My past is not my future. That was then and this is now. I'm not stuck in the past, and I don't have to stay stuck in the past because I have the power of God in me through Christ. That's the old me—this is the new me. Maybe that's what I used to be, but that's not what I am now, and it's certainly not what I'm going to be. My past is not my future.

You are not bound to perpetuating the past. You will only if you choose to, through resentment. You need to take these steps: Revealing your hurt. Releasing those who've offended you. Replacing old tapes with God's truth. Refocusing on the future. When you do that, you will be able to do what Proverbs 4:25 says: "Look straight ahead with honest confidence. Don't hang your head in shame."

You're never going to get well by yourself. If you could have, you'd have been well by now. And you can't. You need other people. You need support. You need a support group. And the only person to find that in is a loving God who knows all about you and cares about your well-being.

When people hurt deeply, they will do almost anything to stop the hurt. They get stoned. Get drunk. Pop some pills. Go to bed with somebody they don't even know. They'll do almost anything to stop the hurt. You've heard this phrase, which was coined years ago: "How do you spell 'relief?'" Sex? Drugs? Alcohol? Pornography? I want to suggest you spell it Jesus.

The world can only offer you temporary painkillers to relieve that pain. There are three problems with painkillers. One, they don't last. Two, they are addicting. Three, they never solve the problem. So when you come down from that experience, that high, that affair, that fling, or whatever it is, you're still lonely and you still feel ashamed and you still feel bitter and angry and worthless. Stop going to quick fixes. They don't work. Give your life to Jesus Christ. "I am the God who heals." That boyfriend is not the answer. That girlfriend is not the answer. That habit is not the answer. "I am the God who heals."

How do you know when you've been healed? You know you've been healed when you want to start sharing the cure with everybody else. You're not really healed until you come to the fifth step.

Step 5: Reach out to help others.

If you're not there, you're not healed yet. Because that's the fifth step of God's healing process. You've got to redeem your pain. You've got to use your experiences to help other people. That's called ministry. God meant for us to help each other. He can use your pain for good. The Bible says in 2 Corinthians 1: "God comforts us every time we have trouble so when others have trouble we can comfort them with the same comfort that God has given to us." Do you want to start over? You can. It's possible. "When someone becomes a Christian, he is a brand-new person inside. He is not the same anymore. A new life has begun." That's what happens. God says, "Let's just erase the past. Let's put new tapes in the tape recorder."

Some of you have stepped across the line. You've accepted Christ in your heart, but you haven't revealed your hurt. You haven't released those who've offended you. You haven't replaced those old tapes with new truths! So you're still living in your old life even though God's given you the power to have a new life. You need to appropriate that today by taking the steps of recovery. You can begin today. It doesn't matter who you are. It doesn't matter where you've been. It doesn't matter what the scar. It doesn't matter what the sin. It doesn't matter how you fell. Somewhere along the way there's healing for your life. Today.

Pray this in your mind:

Jesus Christ, I realize that You see and You feel all the pain in my heart, the hurt, the resentment, the anger, the guilt, the fear, and the insecurities. You see it all. I desperately need Your healing for my hidden wounds

*and my emotional scars. Today, by faith, I'm taking these
initial steps. Help me to admit the things that have hurt
me, to myself and to You and to at least another person,
the things that I've been ashamed of. Thank You for
bringing me to a safe place where I can do this. Today,
I want to begin the healing process by asking You, Jesus
Christ, to come into my life. I'm going to need Your help
to stop focusing on getting even and instead focus on
getting well. I'm going to need Your help and the help
of others to release those who have hurt me and replace
the old tapes in my mind with Your truths. I want to
refocus on the future and Your plan and purpose for my
life. I look forward to the day that I am so healed that I
am able to help others the way You're going to help me.
Father, I realize I need support today. In Your name, I
pray. Amen.*

—Rev. Dr. William D. Tyree, III
Pastor of First Baptist Church, Berkley
Norfolk, VA

What a word from God! I was conversing with one of
the members of First Baptist Church, and she exclaimed,
"That was just what the doctor ordered!" After hearing the
message, many said it brought much healing to their past
wounds. I knew in another way that God was speaking to
me to share His sermon with the world because it would help
facilitate someone else's healing. When I began to share what
I had preached during the same hour at another church,
they proclaimed that Pastor Tyree and I must have discussed
what our topics would be about on that Sunday but in separate worship centers. The hidden wounds, just like any other
hurts, pains, and sorrows, must be acknowledged if you

want to be healed. If you would come out of hiding and be authentic, God will do the rest.

Again, the first step in the healing process is revealing that you're hurt. Facing your wound straight on is the only way you can become healed. Letting go of those who hurt you can only profit you; but when you embrace something that is not good for you, it tends to hurt you. When you let go of the old things, be ready to receive the new thing God has predestined. He says in the Old Testament, "Remember ye not the former things, neither consider the things of old. Behold, I will do a new thing; now it shall spring forth; shall ye not know it" (Isa. 43:18–19). Then He lets us know in 2 Corinthians 5:17, "Therefore if any man be in Christ, he is a new creature: old things are passed away; behold, all things are become new."

When you accept Him as the new thing in your life, you release past hurts, past wounds, and past memories and prevent them from hindering you because you are no longer who you used to be. Your focus and vision change to the new things and the promises He has made just for you. And with that in mind, you will want to help others who have been in your condition and need to be healed.

Isn't it marvelous that God would take your hidden wound, heal you for His glory, and use it for ministry? That's just like the God I have experienced. I challenge you to turn it over to Him right now.

From the sole of the foot even to the head There is nothing sound in it, Only bruises, welts and raw wounds, Not pressed out or bandaged, Nor softened with oil.

—Isaiah 1:6, NASB

The spirit of a man can endure his sickness, But as for a broken spirit who can bear it?

—Proverbs 18:14, NASB

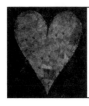

He healeth the broken in heart, and bindeth up their wounds.

—Psalm 147:3

PERSONAL NOTES

_____

_____

_____

_____

_____

_____

_____

_____

_____

CHAPTER 6

WOUNDED HEALERS: PERSONAL TESTIMONIES FROM GOD'S CHOSEN

And they overcame by the blood of the Lamb, and by the word of their testimony; and they loved not their lives unto the death.

—Revelation 12:11

I T'S NOT DIFFICULT to share the power of God when you have experienced Him for yourself. When you are able to share your testimony with someone else, it's an indication that you are healed or on the road to being healed.

The testimonies in this chapter were written by people like you and me. They wanted to express how God healed and delivered them from church hurt and released them with His power to share their stories without fear of judgment. Romans 8:1 says, "There is therefore now no condemnation [guilt] to them which are in Christ Jesus, who do not walk after the flesh, but after the Spirit." Those who have fallen and acknowledged their fall understand Romans 8:1 because they have experienced God's grace. As co-members with them in the body of Christ, we can help them take hold of their healing by refraining from casting judgment on their past. It is important to remember the message of Galatians 6:1, which says, "Brethren, if a man be overtaken in a fault, ye which are spiritual, restore such an one in the spirit of meekness; considering thyself, lest thou also be tempted." If we can practice the ways of God and His Son, Jesus, we will be fulfilling the purpose of the church.

You will find that church hurt is no different from one denomination to another, one ethnic group to another, or one building to another. It seems to be the same drama but with different characters. That's why these testimonies must be shared. The devil is still busy trying to defeat anointed men and women of God to prevent them from fulfilling their predestined purpose. These stories of victory over the devil's strategies must be shared because *exposure is a place of healing*. Most are still hurt because they keep their pain, bitterness, and unforgiveness inside out of fear of rejection from man; but if they realize who they are in Christ, they will see that He will be their protector and the One who continues to open doors for them. It is not who we are but *whose* we are that allows us to stand firm and without fear.

Just Call Me the Wounded Healer

I can truly say I've overcome by the words of my testimony. As you read about my past issue, my spiritual and emotional wound, you may wonder my true identity. I am a European-American woman who thought she had it all together before my issues overwhelmed me. I am now married to a pastor.

We have our own radio ministry and a rapidly growing church in a city in the South.

My name is not important; however, my testimony is. If you read this without a judgmental attitude, you will be able to overcome your wounds, too. If you truly need to identify me, just call me the Wounded Healer. I had to go through a process of transformation in order to understand why I was wounded and how God wanted to heal me. My healing came when I acknowledged that I allowed the self-inflicted pain take residence in my soul and spirit.

My self-inflicted wound began as a very respectful relationship with a very well-known pastor who lived, worshiped, and worked in my city. I knew absolutely nothing of him until I believed God spoke. I had never visited the ministry before, but on my first Sunday there, I was led by the Spirit to join. I began my new member's orientation and saw exactly where I wanted to work in the ministry. Just like every other new member, you wait to be approached to begin work in ministry. Being a woman, you don't want to be too aggressive or assertive—at least that's what I was told. "Your gift will make room for you," they said. In the end, it didn't seem to have mattered if I waited or moved quickly. Well, I did wait, and the knight in shining armor— my pastor—came to me.

I knew the awesome gifts God had given me for ministry. I understood operating in the Spirit and giving Him the glory for all He had endowed me with. I knew and understood the respect that I had for men and women of God in hierarchy in the church. I knew and understood what do, what to say, and how to say it. I was considered a jewel to the ministry.

My pastor thought so, as well. We became very close as we worked many hours together. For months the relationship was innocent, but that all changed in one day.

I have ministered to hundreds of women—black, white, Hispanic, and others—who had relationships with men to whom they were not married. After counseling and ministering to them, my question to God was, how could they be so gullible? Why would they want to put themselves in such an awkward position? I would counsel with a judgmental attitude: "This could never happen to me." I credited myself with always being in control, very independent and knowing and understanding the truths of God's Word. I thought it was enough. What I did not fully understand was my human and emotional side. I did not fully understand that the natural side was craving something I had not experienced in a long time. I never dealt with my issue of loneliness on a natural (emotional) level; it was always a spiritual issue with me. I constantly reminded myself that all I needed was Jesus! But my neglect of my emotions caused an imbalance with my feelings. There was no doubt about it.

However, when I fell into a very deep and adulterous relationship with my pastor, I began to question God about sending me there to be wounded. I blamed everyone except me. I was very angry with God: I felt that He allowed this affair to transpire, because it was He who told me to join the church.

The wound was so deep. It escorted me to a state of depression then led me to have suicidal tendencies. I almost lost my mind—in essence, I did. I allowed this wound to take complete control of my life. When the lusting relationship was over, the pastor couldn't stand me to be there anymore. It was like Amnon after he satisfied his desire with Tamar. (See 2 Samuel 13:1–15.) He no longer desired her. He couldn't stand the sight of her. When my pastor's negative feelings toward me became apparent, I lost all respect for myself. I left the church and didn't return until after a year.

A year before the affair, I had a brief conversation with another woman, an educator like me, at a conference. We exchanged numbers then, and in the midst of my turmoil, God sent her to rescue me.

During our conversation, she gave me a tape that I had never listened to until the day she called. No one had called from the church to see where I was or how I was doing. After all, how could you fail to notice that the children's worship leader and the church and pastor's administrator was missing? But orders had been given to stay away from me: "Don't contact her! She is a cancer in the ministry trying to destroy the vision of God." Oh, yes, I was considered the cancer; the pastor had been in remission until I came to the ministry and his lust lured me into this affair.

The phone rang many times while I was in my depression, but I never answered. I kept the blinds shut, went out only on occasion, ordered food in, and showed up to work only periodically, using vacation and sick time I did not have. I finally lost the job that I had desired for years. My life was messed up, and I was a mess. I lost hope in people who were "holier than thou," and I lost my desire to live. But in the midst of the pain from my wound, I cried out, "What now, God?"

I was at my lowest, feeling sorry for myself and ready to give up my life, when the phone rang. It saved my life. I knew it wasn't the job, because that didn't exist anymore. I knew it wasn't my family, because they ostracized and abandoned me because of the rumor. I knew it wasn't the church, because I had not heard from them in an entire year. I don't even know at this point if I cared who it was, but because I was sick and tired of being sick and tired of where I was and what I had become, I knew I needed help. I wasn't able to reach the phone in time, but I did get the name from caller ID. God gave me a flashback. I remembered my conversation with the woman at the conference, but more importantly, I remembered that my angel had placed a tape in my hand of a message called "The Promise Is in the Purpose, and the Purpose Is in You!"[1]

"Why would I suddenly be reminded of that tape now?" I thought. My past had destroyed my purpose. I didn't feel I was the anointed woman everyone used to know. Still, what did I have to lose? My spirit—what little I had left—urged me to find that tape. It took a while, but I found it and began to listen. The speaker read Isaiah 61:7, "For your shame ye shall have double; and for confusion they shall rejoice in their portion." Then she said she read *In Pursuit of Purpose* by Dr. Myles Monroe. She quoted him: "God's purpose for your past or your present does not hinder your life. Purpose transforms mistakes into miracles and disappointments into testimonies."[2]

I still wasn't convinced I had anything to offer after such a wound, but I listened to the tape. It really was as if the speaker was speaking directly to me to get up from my pity party and get back into a relationship with God. Every word was meant for me. It was my story being told through her message. I wanted to live again, but didn't know how.

I wanted to be healed, but didn't know to whom to turn. I felt God has forsaken me. I felt no one else loved me or even cared. But then I realized that God, in His infinite wisdom, sent the woman at the conference to help me. Was I ready to start the healing process? Not really. But I returned the woman's call. My prayer was that she wouldn't answer, but when she didn't, I felt hopeless again, wanting to crawl back under my rock in darkness, never to come out. That was my last chance. However, God knew where I was and how I wanted to end it. The phone rang again, and it was my angel. She invited me to meet with her for lunch. I began to pretend all was well and that my life since our last meeting a year ago was moving in such an upscale direction. What I didn't know was what God had shared with her about my situation.

The day came and we met. She had a bewildered look on her face when I walked up to her. I guess she saw that my countenance had aged, and I wasn't the vibrant, energetic woman she had met a year ago. I had changed. I looked different. The glow was gone! I didn't even feel anointed. I couldn't even look at her when she spoke. She finally said, "You have a story to tell, and God said it would be in my book." I asked, "Why me?" She said, "Because God does not want to lose such an awesome investment." She admitted that she didn't know what the story was, but that God told her there was a wounded healer who would share her testimony.

When I acknowledged the pain, the wound, the depression, the frustration, and the suicidal thoughts I had experienced in those twelve months, I felt God's Spirit center Himself in my soul. There came a release right in that restaurant. That began my healing process and my road to being a wounded healer. I had to share to save other women who had been called, appointed, and anointed by God, but became severely wounded in the process.

My obedience to share this testimony not only saved my life, but hundreds of other women just like me. If you have been where I was, God wants to heal you. It may not have been an affair with your pastor. Perhaps you experienced rejection, denial, fornication, backbiting, molestation, or rape from someone in leadership in the church. Whatever it is, don't allow it to fester and cause bitterness, resentment, unforgiveness, or shame to linger in your life. Deal with it properly! Let God heal you so that you can stop blaming others and go forth in the name of Jesus.

In my transition

I understand it now. God was using all of it for my good. My frustrations, trials, and tribulations—even my feelings of rejection in ministry and my decision to lash out at others— worked for my good. Romans 8:28 affirms it all: "And we know that all things work together for good to them that love God, to them who are the called according to his purpose." Where I am today is a testimony to it all working together for good, because I do love God. After much waiting on God to move me from hurt to healed, I was angry. Nonetheless, I did not want to allow the church hurt that I endured to separate me from the love of Christ. The Lord brought to my remembrance a passage that I read when I was going through a storm in my earlier years of ministry. Paul clearly states in Acts 14:22 (NIV), "Strengthening the disciples and encouraging them to remain true to the faith. 'We must go through many hardships to enter the kingdom of God.'" My spirit was crushed, but it was not destroyed. Church hurt *did* deter, distract, and debilitate my desires to stay in the race. In the end, though, my faith was strengthened and my heart was encouraged! I won! I pressed through the pain to my purpose.

FROM VICTIM TO VICTOR

Wanting to be like Jesus hurts! I don't care what anyone says; it hurts. I say to myself, "If I had known then what I know now, I may have never prayed the prayer, 'All I want to be is like Jesus.'" When I was chosen to go through the test, I had not yet realized the magnitude of God's grace or the suffering of His Son. After the pain of my trial, I heard a sermon that permeated my spirit. I will never forget what the preacher said.

> *Then those Roman soldiers...take Jesus and they scourged Him (Isaiah 53). All the while this was happening, He did not even open His mouth. He is going to obey the will of the Father. Those Roman soldiers stripped Jesus naked. They began to mock Him. They put a purple robe on Him. They took a crown of thorns and crushed it in His skull. Think about those thorn bushes crushed into His skull. They spit in His face. Then they beat Him, and they beat Him, and they beat Him. Isaiah 52 says that His visage, His face, and His body was so beaten, bruised, and disfigured that He hardly resembled a human. In other words, you have*

a total blood lynching. You have a mob who beats Him and no one pulls them off. They beat Him within an inch of His life. The beating is so bad that He cannot carry the cross. He does not have any strength left after receiving such brutal punishment.[1]

After replaying that sermon in my mind, my personal trial took me back to read and re-read every episode of Jesus being denied, betrayed, and crucified because I was denied, betrayed, and emotionally crucified. He lived to tell about, and so did I. That's the kind of God I serve.

Listen, when you pray, be ready to receive what you have prayed for, and not in the way you request it. God has already chosen your plan, and it will not cater to anyone else's life, faith, or character except yours. What you have gone through or what you are in the midst of now was tailor-made just for you. All you have to do is keep the faith and know that God has already declared you a victor because the Word says in 1 Corinthians 10:13, "There hath no temptation taken you but such as is common to man: but God is faithful, who will not suffer you to be tempted above that ye are able; but will with the temptation also make a way to escape, that ye may be able to bear it." Now, aren't you glad that you did not give up in the midst of the storm? You can see I didn't give up because I am able to share my testimony today of being a victim to becoming a victor.

Yes, even in the midst of my trial I still wanted to be like Jesus, healing the sick, feeding the hungry, clothing the naked, and even counseling those who were infirm in their minds. I knew I could help them to see that Jesus was all they needed. Well, it didn't work like that. I was ready to throw in the towel, and had even written my letter of resignation as church administrator and scheduled a meeting with the pastor. That day I had called it quits in the church. Then I met this preacher who had a word from God. It was God-appointed.

I knew her, but she did not know me. I had attended many conferences with my wife where the lady was preaching. When we met, I shared with her that a message she had preached helped me to realize that some of what I was going through was my own fault. She said, "Stop blaming everyone else for your problem and take the blame for yourself. Stop being the *victim* and declare yourself a *victor.*" We laughed, and she began to share the rest of that sermon, which lead me to tell her my plight.

When I first began working in the ministry it had less than two hundred members, but it had grown to nearly 2,500 in the ten years I had been there. I continued my fellowship there because of the anointing I witnessed on the preacher's life and because the Word of God was being taught and preached. After several months of attending, the Lord led me to covenant with this church. My wife refused to join with me.

It was a few years before I found myself involved in the daily operation of the church. I became the administrator, and things for the ministry began to grow in organization and structure. Besides, we were in the process of building a new sanctuary and adding on as the vision of the church was manifested through the pastor. I enjoyed helping people. It was a love that I thought nothing and no one could ever take away. I was excited and knew the ministry could only go up—until the devil, after departing for a season (Lk. 4:13), showed up again. It was just like him to be on the job.

Church hurt took away my desire to give myself to others as Jesus gave Himself for other people. Have you been a victim? There are many definitions for *victim*. *Webster's Dictionary* defines it as: "(1) one who suffers injury, loss, or death because of a voluntary undertaking; (2) one tricked, swindled, or taken advantage of; (3) one harmed by or made to suffer from an act, circumstance, agency [such as the church] or condition."[3] Yes, I was a victim in every sense of the definition. I felt it was written on my forehead.

During my involvement with the ministry, when someone needed an ear or a person to release their cares to, I was chosen. I can't understand why I was always chosen, because I felt I was one of the most judgmental persons in the church. Nevertheless, folks came to me anyway. Some of you would never admit that you judge people and struggle to love unconditionally. Well, since I'm free, I can share that with you. Thank God for deliverance.

I could not believe the things people would share or how they could get so caught up in certain situations. As I listened, I became a part of the drama. You don't have to be directly involved in sin or strife to allow yourself to get immersed in it, and if you're in it, before long you become it. That's what happened to me. When I found myself listening to the stories, some of which seemed to be out of a novel, I was at the point of hating the church and hating people in the church. Hearing their stories brought back so many negative memories of who I used to be. I was hearing *their* stories, but I saw myself in the plot.

I finally realized that I had made some poor choices with people and blamed others when, in reality, it was my fault. The names of the characters changed, but not my situation. I was always blaming others because it was the easiest thing to do.

I had been hanging out with the wrong church people, people who wanted to run the sheep away. Yes, they do exist, wolves in fancy sheep's clothing—beautiful hats, expensive suits, and nice cars, with eloquent speech, Fortune 500 occupations, and homes in neighborhoods some only dream about. Oh, yes! They're in your church, too, and you may be worshiping right beside one of them.

My pastors were great people, a man and woman of character and integrity. They always shared much wisdom in regard to my being such a great listener to the congregants. Much of what they shared, though, I did not apply. It felt good being considered a confidant, until one day the devil showed himself. After the very people I was helping in the church accused me of trying to get rid of the pastor by spreading vicious rumors about him, I could not take it any longer.

Why me? It's amazing that people want what you have but are not willing to go through the trial you went through to get it. I had suffered for the position I had in the church and someone else wanted it, so I became the main character in their play. My joy over being a confidant turned sour because I enjoyed the attention. I was pulled into the arena of negative talk about the two people I respected the most: my pastor and his wife. By listening, you're guilty by association. I kept hearing my grandmother say, "Pride comes before the fall." Yes, I was proud that people looked up to me. They came to me for all kinds of advice. Some even bypassed the pastor and his wife just to talk to me. That felt good. Then one day, the enemy showed up. And so did God.

God came to me in a vision, and when I heard Him, I picked up my journal and began to write. There were two things I clearly heard Him say: "The *victor* speaks power," and, "The *victor* lets go in order to get up."

Was I surprised to hear that from God? No, because He will speak when you are ready to listen and obey. After I had made up in my mind that I was truly tired of being the victim, I cried out to God and He answered my prayer. I ran like Elijah to a cave and hid myself there. I was in despair and began to cry out to God once again. And when I came out of the cave, I was a new creature. Old things were passed away and, behold, I knew without a shadow of a doubt that I was a new creature in Christ. I began to search the Scriptures to apply His Word to my life. My motto became "The power is in what I say and believe." The scriptures I found became living testaments to my daily life. When I awakened in the morning, I would speak them. When I took my lunch break, I would speak them. When I had an appointment with clients, I would speak them. When I went to a church meeting, I would speak them. When I went to bed every night, I would speak them. They have become my life because they resurrected the promises of God that I had buried because of my wounds. If you know that there is power in your words to become the victor, then I pray that you will speak words of life over them. I share them with you knowing that you, too, can walk in them—but you have to know the God you serve and what you mean to Him.

First, you truly matter to God! You are valuable in His sight. I had to recognize that while I was being hurt by church people. My mind really had to shift to what God had already said about who He created. After He created me, Scripture says in Genesis 1:31, "And God saw every thing that he had made, and, and, behold, it was very good." Then in the New Testament James 1:17 states, "Every good and perfect gift is from above, and cometh down from the Father of lights, with whom is no variableness, neither shadow of turning." Finally, to help you understand who you are to God and nothing you ever do or what people do to you will turn you away from him, Ephesians 2:10 lets you know, "For we are His workmanship, created in Christ Jesus unto good works, which God hath before ordained that we should walk in them."

You see, others may not think you matter or are valuable, but what they think really should not matter to you. They did not create you, nor did you create yourself, for the Bible declares in Psalm 100:3, "It is he that hath made us, and not we ourselves." I found out that to be a victor meant my faith and character would be tested—and it was. When God showed me my own strength in the midst of adversity, I began to see myself as the victor and not the victim, but it was not before I endured the hurt from the church that I realized "the joy of the LORD is your strength" (Neh. 8:10).

Speak out

So what do I do now? I speak words of power, and you can, too. These scriptures helped me realize the power God had given me through my tongue to speak His words and promises over my life. Read these scriptures and allow them to help you.

> *Death and life are in the power of the tongue: and they that love it shall eat the fruit thereof.*
> —Proverbs 18:21

Or take ships as an example. Although they are so large and are driven by strong winds, they are steered by a very small rudder wherever the pilot wants to go. Likewise the tongue is a small part of the body, but it makes great boasts. Consider what a great forest is set on fire by a small spark.

—James 3:4–5, NIV

Nay, in all these things we are more than conquerors through him that loved us.

—Romans 8:37

For verily I say unto you, That whosoever shall say unto this mountain, Be thou removed, and be thou cast into the sea; and shall not doubt in his heart, but shall believe that those things which he saith shall come to pass; he shall have whatsoever he saith.

—Mark 11:23

Beat your plowshares into swords, and your pruning-hooks into spears: let the weak say, I am strong.

—Joel 3:10

Ye are of God, little children, and have overcome them: because greater is he that is in you, than he that is in the world.

—1 John 4:4

No weapon that is formed against thee shall prosper; and every tongue that shall rise against thee in judgment thou shalt condemn. This is the heritage of the servants of the LORD, and their righteousness is of me, saith the LORD.

—Isaiah 54:17

WOUNDED BUT NOT HINDERED TO WORSHIP

I (Angela Corprew-Boyd) believe the world needs to recognize that if you have been hurt in church as much as I have and have survived, then it's important to recognize the role of God's power in the healing process. I am a living testament that no matter how many weapons form against you—be it first ladies, jealous ministers, pastors, deacon boards, mothers of the church, choir members, ushers, associate ministers, you name it—they will not prosper if you have been appointed, anointed, sanctified, and ordained by God! I'm still here because of His power, which resides in me. This is my personal testimony.

There was a time in my life when I found myself in a place where I had grown expeditiously. God was doing quick work in me, and I was making myself available and accessible for His glory. But leadership didn't see it that way. I had worked diligently, faithfully, and purposefully with the intent to help unveil the vision of the church. However, when God called me to establish Women Empowered in the Millennium, a women's ministry, turbulent storms began to hover over my head. Leadership didn't recognize that it was from God even after I felt He had given confirmation because they were not listening to His voice.

The first year of Women Empowered, the ministry was thriving and the support from leadership was astounding. I couldn't believe that God would use someone like me to begin a good and mighty work for the kingdom, but I was grateful He chose me. The second year, we had our second women's conference, and it was a success. However, the devil became angry—so angry that I was put on the spot in church one night. Can you imagine sitting in the midst of more than three hundred people and *you're* the subject of the message? Well, I've been there. How embarrassing. I sat there that night and listened to each word as it penetrated my heart: "You think you're somebody just because God has established your ministry. I want you to know it's not going anywhere unless I affirm it. You come in here sitting in the pulpit with an attitude because you think you know something. Your degrees don't mean anything. Who do you think you are? You can leave the church if you want to. And if you do leave, that only lets me know you have a demon in you."

Oh, the congregation was clapping and jeering and standing with loud "Hallelujahs" and "Yes, pastor, tell it like it is." I thought to myself, "This sounds so rehearsed." It was as if a play were going on, and the cast had already been selected—but I didn't get a part. Needless to say, it was because I was the subject of the drama that particular night, the object of ridicule.

The pastor began to attack my personal ministry. I had confided in him about an awesome testimony of deliverance a woman at the conference shared with me. God had delivered her from lesbianism, and she began to sing the praises of God for Women Empowered in the Millennium. God spoke to me the night she shared her testimony and said, "This is another issue that your ministry will embrace and lead people to deliverance." I said, "Yes, Lord." However, on that terrible night at church, what came out of the pastor's mouth next simply astonished me. I was in shock. He said, "If you keep going in the direction you are, you are going to be a lesbian yourself," a reference to the testimony I had shared with him in confidence. He was pointing directly at me. I could not believe it. What trust was lost. The pastor then asked me to speak what was in my spirit because he felt God had given me a word. Oh, my heart was pierced. I could not move. I was paralyzed in my pain. I heard the Lord say, "Pray." When I began to pray, I felt a powerful wave of God's anointing cover me, and He said, "Fear not, for I am with you." I felt like Mary when Gabriel visited her. I was carrying an anointed seed and it was being birthed in the place of my rejection.

I know many of you are wondering, "Did you give the word to the church?" Oh, yes. It was a mind game that was being played. That's why you have to know God for yourself. It wasn't a prophetic word from God—just Angie speaking from her heart. I knew that, the pastor knew that, and I was praying that the people of God knew that. After all was said and done, and the pastor was convicted and called the very enemies who constantly attacked me to come and embrace me. It struck me as just another sideshow.

I was determined I would not let them win this battle. I was stubborn, and I came back the next night—only to get another tongue-lashing from the preacher. This time he said, "I don't care if you leave. We don't need you, because we have survived this long." It was evident that something had been said previously because it seemed everyone knew exactly who the preacher was talking about once again. I was amazed but determined that he would not run me away. Was my mind on the service? Of course not! I was emotionally wounded, in despair, heartbroken. I wanted to hide under the pew.

I respected this man of God. There was nothing that I would not have done for the ministry. I was the administrator when my expertise was needed on professional matters or when the finances of the ministry were decreasing. You always knew there would be a word when the preacher needed something from you. He would manipulate the congregation from the pulpit. My prayer was that he would change, and I believed God for that because of the awesome anointing that was on his life. I sat under that ministry for five years, though God had instructed me to leave sooner. I got all that God had predestined for me, but when I look back over the situation, I can see that I should have left when God spoke. I allowed myself to be inflicted with unnecessary pain by staying past my time and disobeying God. At the time I said it was my compassion for the pastor's ministry and the other people serving under him that caused me to stay, but that was an excuse to make myself feel better. It was really fear that clutched my heart and had me paralyzed.

Pain from a wound will affect not just your emotional state, but it can produce sickness and debilitate you from wanting to ever go back to church. Anger, bitterness, and resentment had reached maturation in me. I was finished with church and church folks, but God would not let me go. In spite of my wounds and my disobedience in remaining under that pastor's ministry, God spoke to me through a word that my pastor preached. He said, "Stop protecting your feelings and protect your future. Hurt is trying to rob you of your promise." I also heard him say, "If you are going to progress, you have to move past your past." I thought about Paul in Philippians 3:13–14, "Brethren, I count not myself to have apprehended: but this one thing I do, forgetting those things which are behind, and reaching forth unto those things which are before, I press toward the mark for the prize of the high calling of God in Christ Jesus."

My freedom came when I began to worship God and release my spirit from being wounded. In all that I endured, it's a testimony to God's power at work in me that I was still able to worship Him. It was the power of worship that kept my mind on Him and not my wound. However, I knew God was telling me that I had to forgive in order to have the strength to press on through the rest of the healing process. He brought the Word back to my remembrance. I went to Matthew 5:22–24 and read, "But I say unto you, That whosoever is angry with his brother without a cause shall be in danger of the judgment: and whosoever shall say to his brother, Raca, shall be in danger of the council: but whosoever shall say, Thou fool, shall be in danger of hell fire. Therefore if thou bring thy gift to the altar, and there rememberest that thy brother hath ought against thee; Leave there thy gift before the altar, and go thy way; first be reconciled to thy brother, and then come and offer thy gift."

I took the first step of obedience and returned to the place my wound was inflicted to ask for forgiveness. I know you may be asking why I asked for forgiveness from the person who wounded me. I had to make it right if I was going to move from wound to witness, so I did. Today I can say I am free. John 8:36 says, "If the Son makes you free, you shall be free indeed" (John 8:36, NKJV).

You will not be free until you ask for forgiveness and let it go. Allow God to heal you so that you may transform from being the wounded to being a witness. Don't allow your church hurt to monopolize your life. Move forward!

When God appointed others to my life for me to minister to, I had no idea that I would be shepherding them through the very issues that had plagued my life—wounds from church hurt. God helped me to overcome much of what I was dealing with in my spirit through ministry to others. I could be there for others because God had been there for me.

It's been a challenge, but I am a survivor! I've always wanted to fit in, but I could not. When I accepted my call to ministry, I simply wanted to please God. I was willing to do whatever He had called me to do. I wasn't the only one who realized that was my desire. My father told me on many occasions that my compassion for people would be my downfall. At the time, I didn't understand what he meant. I fell, but through the grace of God I was able to get back up again.

And the LORD God will wipe tears from off all faces.
                                                          —Isaiah 25:8

From the sole of the foot—unto the head, There is no soundness in it, Wound, and bruise, and fresh smiting! They have not been closed nor bound, Nor have they softened with ointment.

—Isaiah 1:6, RYL

The spirit of a man sustaineth his sickness, And a smitten spirit who doth bear?

—Proverbs 18:14, RYL

Create in me a clean heart, O God; and renew a right spirit within me. Cast me not away from thy presence; and take not thy holy spirit from me. Restore unto me the joy of thy salvation; and uphold me with thy free spirit.

—Psalm 51:10–12

PERSONAL NOTES

_____

_____

_____

_____

_____

_____

_____

_____

_____

_____

CHAPTER 7

THE PATH TO HEALING

I CAN'T BE MYSELF when I am in pain. I can't be myself when I am fighting frustration. I can't be myself if I am mired by hurt. Why? Because the real me is calling to come out. The real me wants to be used by God. The real me is ready to give in to His plan, whatever it may bring. The intimate, private, secret me needs to be healed. My soul is crying out.

What is your spirit telling you? Haven't you felt your soul crying out to God? Isn't it time to move forth in the glory of God and let your inner being be revealed? Of course it is. If there is a great deal of hidden hurt in your life that you can't let go, the time is now.

Your inner being—your genuine identity—is waiting to come out. Don't allow your pain to steal your joy. Don't allow your frustration to overtake your peace. Don't allow your hurt to prolong the wait for your blessing. It's time to be healed by the power of the most high God. It's time to stop pursuing the illusion of comfort in spite of your wound-edness and get real with God. He wants you to trust and depend on the power of the precious Holy Ghost to give you joy and peace. He wants you to desire Him so that you move to another level of His anointing and power.

It's time to expose the hidden wound. Take the bandage off and give it air, the Word of God who is Jesus the Christ. What are you waiting for? Let the healing begin!

You Shall Be Healed

The first step you take on the path to healing may feel the hardest: you must acknowledge the hurt, the sorrow, the embarrassment, and even the shame of what you have experienced. Be honest with yourself about what dwells inside, hinders your true praise, and degrades who you really are. Once you sincerely acknowledge the pain, you must go to God to allow Him to destroy the guilt that hinders your spiritual growth. His delivering power will endow you with a renewed mind, a clean heart, and the right spirit to allow your true identify to come forth. You will—not may, not might, but *will*—be healed. No hurt is too great for the Master! No pain is too severe for the Healer! No frustration is too much for God to conquer!

Now that you have read this book, I encourage you to give your wounds to God. Don't allow the hurt in your inner self to destroy you. Be willing to let God heal the hidden hurt so that you can fulfill your destined purpose in Him. Once your inner self is healed, you will be an effective and productive servant for God. Let God restore you and heal your inner being so that you can begin your new life.

Isaiah 43:18–20 gives us an important word from the Lord about our healing: "Remember ye not the former things, neither consider the things of old. Behold, I will do a new thing; now it shall spring forth; shall ye not know it? I will even make a way in the wilderness, and rivers in the desert." When you release your past and stop considering what could or should have been, you are on your way to being healed.

ONE QUESTION

Imagine this: how would it feel if you had freedom from your past? How would it feel if you had freedom from your disappointments, problems, and failures? How would it feel to have freedom from your hurts, pains, and sorrow? What about from the source of the problem, your wounds? Wouldn't you feel lighter? Energized?

No one can promise you'll be richer or smarter or prettier, but God can offer you joy and a peace that passes all understanding. It's your choice. Psalm 118:24 says, "This is the day which the LORD hath made; we will rejoice and be glad in it." It's time to rejoice! Isn't this what you really want?

To take your first step on the road to deliverance, pray the following prayer with me:

Father, You said in Revelation 3:20, "Behold, I stand at the door, and knock: if any man hear my voice, and open the door, I will come in to him, and will sup with him, and he with me." I have seen You standing and have heard You knocking, but I was distracted by my wounds and did not open. First, I am sorrowful for not understanding that You are the Creator of every good and perfect gift and that I am a gift from You. Second, I am sorrowful for not recognizing You as my personal healer. Right now, Father, I dismiss every noise that would clog my ears from hearing Your knock. I speak against every and any thing that would block my vision from seeing You stand at my door. I am asking You to come in now. My heart is bleeding for You, Lord. Come in now. I want to know what it feels like to be free of church hurt, free of chaos and confusion, and free to praise You with the right spirit. I want You to sup with me now; I want to experience communion with you. I am opening the door of my wound and removing the many bandages so that Your Spirit can breathe on me, heal me, and set me free. Breathe on my wounds! I am calling out wounds from depression, rejection, failed relationships, divorce, adultery, fornication, envy, lying, backbiting, homosexuality, abortion, and low self-esteem. I am making myself available to You, God, to deliver and use me for Your glory.

Here I am. Heal me. In your name, Jesus. Amen!

And when Jesus saw her, he called her to him, and said unto her, Woman, thou art loosed from thine infirmity.

—Luke 13:12

PERSONAL NOTES

_____

_____

_____

_____

_____

_____

_____

_____

MY FAVORITE PASSAGES

MY HEALING PROCESS may be different from yours, but God and the Scriptures never change. These passages were dear to my heart during my quiet times with God as I walked through my healing. Every day I would meditate on them, and they would act as salve to my simple abrasions and soothe my deepest cuts. As I read and meditated over them daily, these passages brought healing to my wound and the excruciating pain that came with it. These scriptures will help you heal, too, so that you can be a wounded healer.

> *He healeth the broken in heart, and bindeth up their wounds.*
>
> —Psalm 147:3

> *He sent His word, and healed them, and delivered them from their destructions.*
>
> —Psalm 107:20

> *He sent forth his word and healed them; he rescued them from the grave.*
>
> —Psalm 107:20, NIV

> *My wounds grow foul and fester because of my foolishness.*
>
> —Psalm 107:20, RSV

The spirit of a man will sustain his infirmity; but a wounded spirit who can bear?

—Proverbs 18:14

The human spirit can endure a sick body, but who can bear a crushed spirit?

—Proverbs 18:14, NLT

For I will restore health unto thee, and I will heal thee of thy wounds, saith the LORD; because they called thee an Outcast, saying, This is Zion, whom no man seeketh after.

—Jeremiah 30:17

For I will apply a bandage unto thee, and I will heal thee of thy wounds, saith Jehovah; for they have called thee an outcast: This is Zion that no man seeketh after.

—Jeremiah 30:17, DT

[The good Samaritan, an example of Christ] went to him, and bound up his wounds, pouring in oil and wine, and set him on his own beast, and brought him to an inn, and took care of him.

—Luke 10:34

ABOUT THE AUTHOR

Angela Corprew-Boyd has always been one to set her mind on things she hoped for, knowing that God was able to perform them. The eighth child of ten, she didn't allow the negative statistics she heard as she was growing up to hinder her from pursuing her destiny. Understanding what a mighty seed she was carrying, she allowed God to anoint and appoint her to do His will. She has adopted Philippians 1:6 as her motto: "Being confident of this very thing, that he which has begun a good work in you will complete it until the day of Jesus Christ" (KJV).

With a passion to see and assist God's people to walk in their purpose, she has an anointed fervor to teach and preach the unadulterated truths of God's Word through the two ministries God led her to start; Women Empowered in the Millennium, Inc. and Angela Corprew-Boyd Ministries, Inc. Praying that they will embrace what will escort them to their destiny, Angela's desire is that men and women isolate their pain from their pursuit of purpose while "forgetting those things which are behind, and reaching forth unto those things which are before" (Phil. 3:13). She impresses upon her listeners the need to unmask themselves and confront both who they really are and the real-life issues trying to keep them from fulfilling their dreams.

Since the inception of her ministries, Angela has traveled nationally as well as to London, Africa, and Jamaica to teach and preach the gospel and to serve as a conference consultant. Her Empowered Leadership Training Sessions have allowed her to minister to deacons, pastors, and missionaries; men, women and youth; and at the annual Virginia Union University Samuel DeWitt School of Theology Leadership Training Conference. She is also the author and publisher of *Preparation for the Ultimate Purpose: If I Perish, Let Me Perish, But I'm Next!*

The Lord has also afforded Angela the opportunity to pursue higher education. She received a bachelor of science degree in English with a minor in speech from Old Dominion University in Norfolk, Virginia. Her master's degree in urban education/administration and personnel management was obtained from Norfolk State University, and her doctoral degree in strategic leadership is from Regent University in Virginia Beach, Virginia. She is an assistant principal in the Chesapeake public schools system and an adjunct professor at Norfolk State University. She was ordained elder in the gospel ministry, and God appointed her to the staff at First Baptist Church, Berkley, in Norfolk, Virginia, as the assistant to the pastor, the Reverend Dr. William D. Tyree, III.

Dr. Corprew-Boyd is married to Reginald Boyd, and they are the proud parents of Devin, Donovan, and Dawn. She wants people to know that everything that she has accomplished professionally, educationally, and spiritually is because of what God has predestined for her life. She accepted it, walked in His will for it, and gives God the glory and the honor for all of it. She has opened her heart, mind, and soul as an empty vessel waiting patiently to be used by God.

NOTES

CHAPTER 1
NO LONGER BOUND

1. *The Nelson Study Bible* (Nashville, TN: Thomas Nelson Publishers, 1997).

CHAPTER 4
RESENTMENTS

1. *American Medical Association Complete Medical Encyclopedia* (New York: Random House, 2003).

2. Finis Jennings Dake, *Dake Annotated Reference Bible* (Lawrenceville, GA: Dake Publishing, 1996).

3. *American Medical Association Complete Medical Encyclopedia*

CHAPTER 6
WOUNDED HEALERS

1. Rev. Dr. Peter Wherry, sermon entitled "Seven Last Words." Norfolk, VA, April 2005.

2. Myles Monroe, *In Pursuit of Purpose* (Shippensburg, PA: Destiny Image, 1992).

3. *Random House School Dictionary of the English Language*, unabridged edition (New York: Random House, 1978).

OTHER BOOKS BY
DR. ANGELA CORPREW-BOYD

IF I PERISH, LET ME PERISH, BUT I'M NEXT!

Where would you be without Esther? God chose Esther to help women today realize the importance of their purpose and position for "such a time as this!" Esther went against political power, tradition, her comfort zone, and fear to save a nation. If she had not gone to see the king, would the Jews have been destroyed? Would the Son of God have come? We read in Esther 4:14 (NKJV) that her uncle reminded her, "If you remain completely silent at this time, relief and deliverance will arise for the Jews from another place, but you and your father's house will perish. Yet who knows whether you have come to the kingdom for such a time as this?" Thank God for Esther recognizing not only her purpose but also the power of her position. Have you recognized yours?